Reclaiming Democratic Education

Reclaiming Democratic Education

Student and Teacher Activism and the Future of Education Policy

Christopher D. Thomas

TEACHERS COLLEGE PRESS

TEACHERS COLLEGE | COLUMBIA UNIVERSITY
NEW YORK AND LONDON

Published by Teachers College Press,® 1234 Amsterdam Avenue, New York, NY 10027

Copyright © 2022 by Teachers College, Columbia University

Front cover design by Pete Donahue. Illustration by Николай Григорьев / Adobe Stock.

Library of Congress Cataloging-in-Publication Data is available at loc.gov

ISBN 978-0-8077-6690-3 (paper)
ISBN 978-0-8077-6691-0 (hardcover)
ISBN 978-0-8077-8100-5 (ebook)

Printed on acid-free paper
Manufactured in the United States of America

I'd like to dedicate this book to Elizabeth Kane, whose love and support made this possible, and to the student and teacher activists herein who, in the words of Congressman John Lewis, are making "good trouble, necessary trouble."

Contents

Acknowledgments

Looking back, this book feels inevitable. The pieces fell into place and an accident of timing offered the perfect subject. But nothing about my educational odyssey or career was predetermined. Instead, every idea here, every decision I made in my educational journey and career, can be traced back to my amazing teachers, professors, and classmates. You all challenged me, pushed me, and helped me see the power of education. I could never have gotten here or written this without you. Frank Beickelman, T.K. Daniel, Antoinette Errante, Valerie Kinloch, Debra Moddelmog, Beverly Moss, Jan Nespor, and Timothy San Pedro: Many of the ideas and thoughts in this work you will find deeply familiar. Your classes and our conversations were where these ideas first took form and where the larger arc of this project took shape.

I am also deeply indebted to my PhD candidacy exam committee, Ann Allen, Jackie Blount, Daniel Tokaji, and Bryan Warnick, for giving focus and direction to this project. In addition, this project would not be what it is without the thoughtful and encouraging support of my dissertation committee: Ann Allen, Jackie Blount, and Bryan Warnick. Your guidance and feedback have shaped this project very much for the better. To my advisor, Bryan Warnick, thank you for modeling how to be a thoughtful, objective, and critical scholar who never loses sight of the practical significance and real-world impact of our work. Because of your mentoring, I am excited to be on my way toward following your example. Additionally, to all my teachers, classmates, and students, thank you all for showing me what education can—and should—be. You, like the student and teacher activists discussed here, are already the active policy agents that educational policy so sorely needs.

I would also like to express a huge thank you to my family and friends for all their love and support. I'd like to specially thank my very talented sister, Brittany Horner, who created the timeline of student and teacher activism that you'll see in Chapter 1, and Aaron Rothey for offering thoughtful feedback and encouragement on earlier drafts. Finally, a sincere thank you to everyone at Teachers College Press for all their assistance and work in making this book what it is, especially Emily Spangler for her insightful questions and suggestions throughout the process and John Bylander for his incomparable attention to detail. To everyone: I could never have done this without your help and constant encouragement. Thank you!

CHAPTER 1

Student and Teacher Civic Activism and the Future of Education Policy

Since 2011, the United States has experienced significant protest movements and societal unrest. From the Occupy Wall Street and Tea Party movements of the early 2010s to the more recent Women's March and Black Lives Matter movements, it seems that no segment of American society has been untouched by this trend. American education is no exception. Student and teacher activism has similarly been on the rise, climbing to levels not seen since the "decade of protest" in the 1960s and early 1970s. Since the spring of 2018, hundreds of thousands—if not millions—of students, teachers, and their allies have engaged in civic activism across the United States.

These students and teachers continue long traditions of civic activism by these groups. Indeed, student and teacher activists have repeatedly shaped the course of history. Around the world, students have initiated and been integral participants in revolutions, uprisings, and cultural upheavals (Boren, 2001). Teachers, for their part, have often supported students in these endeavors and have been a powerful political force in their own right. In the United States, students and teachers have led antiwar protests, protested against climate change and environmental harm, spearheaded abolitionist and civil rights movements, and agitated for greater legal rights and recognition—among many other causes. While these activities are often associated with postsecondary students and professors, K–12 students and teachers have their own histories of activism. Contemporary primary and secondary student activists and their teachers are the direct descendants of these traditions.

The spring of 2018 saw the greatest concentration of student protests and teacher strikes in the United States since the 1960s and early 1970s. The students of 2018 were commemorating the victims of school shootings and protesting against gun violence and its impact on their schools. Of particular importance for these students was the shooting at Marjory Stoneman Douglas High School in Parkland, Florida. In a nation where mass shootings are increasingly common, the Parkland shooting was another in a long line of shootings, many of which have occurred at schools (Cohen et al., 2014). Yet, in the wake of this tragedy, the students of Parkland and their allies led massive protests and demonstrations across the United States throughout the spring of 2018. In the months of March, April, and May, hundreds of thousands of students and concerned citizens walked out of their schools, took to the streets, and marched throughout the country to protest against gun violence and commemorate its victims.

At the same time that students across the country were protesting against gun violence, many of America's teachers were also engaging in civic activism. During the spring of 2018, West Virginia, Kentucky, Oklahoma, Arizona, Colorado, and North Carolina all experienced statewide teacher strikes, many of which coincided with statewide teacher protests and school closures. These strikes were situated within their particular social and political context and were in response to different—though related—issues. Teachers in West Virginia were protesting stagnant wages and rising health care costs. Teachers in Kentucky protested changes to teacher pensions and benefits. The teachers in Oklahoma, Arizona, Colorado, and North Carolina were protesting severe and recurring cuts to education budgets that impacted teacher and staff salaries as well as the quality of students' education. All of these strikes involved teachers banding together to have their voices heard in an attempt to impact educational policy.

While the student and teacher activists during the spring of 2018 were responding to different issues, their activities are highly interconnected in two important ways. It was not merely an accident of timing that saw both students and teachers protesting at levels unseen since the 1960s. First, these protests continue a long and interconnected history of student and teacher civic activism in the United States. Both students and teachers have strong activist traditions, and these traditions are deeply intertwined. These histories demonstrate that students and teachers have drawn inspiration, strength, goals, and strategies from each other while also pursuing their own political aims. Additionally, these activities have been deeply rooted in larger societal civic movements, with student and teacher activism extending, being understood within, and sometimes even leading these larger movements. The student and teacher activists during the spring of 2018— and since—continue this long tradition.

Second, these seemingly dissimilar activities are connected by the ways in which contemporary educational policy positions students and teachers. These students and teachers were engaging in civic activism in an era of education policy that actively undermines their ability to influence and impact what happens in schools. While students were expressly protesting against gun violence in schools and teachers were striking against systemic under- and disinvestments in schools, each group was also implicitly resisting and speaking back to an educational policy paradigm, one exemplified by the *A Nation at Risk* report of 1983, that encourages their passivity and silence.

Understanding the deep connections between student protests and teacher strikes, as well as situating these activities within their historical traditions and their contemporary political context, demonstrates the significance of the student and teacher activism that roiled the United States in the spring of 2018—and that continues to do so. In many ways, these contemporary student protests and teacher strikes are more of the same; they continue a long tradition of student and teacher civic activism. And yet, these protests also break the mold. They occurred within an era of educational policy that prioritizes economic competitiveness while neglecting and actively discouraging the civic agency and democratic participation of teachers and students. Exploring these activities, the historical traditions that gave rise to them, and the contemporary policy paradigm within which they occurred demonstrates how student and teacher civic activism constitutes a rejection of the currently dominant A Nation at Risk paradigm and offers a welcome foundation for a competing Education for Citizenship paradigm in educational policy.

THE STUDENT PROTESTS OF THE SPRING OF 2018

The impetus for the student protests of spring 2018 was the tragedy that occurred at Marjory Stoneman Douglas High School (MSD) on February 14, 2018. On that day, a gunman entered his former school and shot and killed 17 people, injuring 17 more. The gunman had been a former student at MSD but, at the time of the shooting, was expelled for disciplinary problems and enrolled at an alternative school in the district (Chuck et al., 2018).

Responses to the shooting were immediate and forceful. Within a few weeks of February 14, students at Parkland as well as other students and their allies across the United States organized three national demonstrations commemorating the victims of gun violence in schools and protesting its effects (Grinberg & Muaddi, 2018; Nir, 2018; Rosenblatt et al., 2018). Over the 3 months that followed the Parkland shooting, hundreds of thousands of students, teachers, and their allies would participate in these and dozens of other protests and activities.

The first protest was planned by the Women's March for March 14, the 1-month anniversary of the Parkland shooting. Titled the #ENOUGH National School Walkouts, this protest involved students walking out of their schools at 10:00 A.M. local time for 17 minutes—1 minute for each victim of the Parkland shooting—to take action against gun violence. According to the Women's March (2019), over 1.6 million students across the United States participated in this protest (Women's March, 2019). The Women's March is a national political activism organization that seeks to "to harness the political power of diverse women and their communities to create transformative social change" (Women's March, n.d.). Founded in 2016, the organization grew out of the Women's March on Washington, DC, that followed the 2016 presidential election. The Women's March takes a broad and intersectional view of women's rights, believing that "women's rights are human rights" (Women's March, n.d.). Because of this encompassing view of women's rights, ending violence is a key tenet of the Women's March, and is what motivated them to organize the #ENOUGH National School Walkouts.

Students from Parkland planned the second national protest, the March for Our Lives, which took place on March 24, 2018. This march saw students and other concerned citizens march on Washington, DC, and other political centers to advocate for gun control regulations. According to the March for Our Lives (n.d.-a) organization, the day of protest was the "largest global protest in history" with "millions coming together . . . to remind the world that young people have the power to drive real change." Focused on youth participation in politics and curbing all forms of gun violence, the March for Our Lives organization has continued to grow and advocate following the March 24 protest.

The third protest, the National School Walkout, started as a Change.org petition by Lane Murdock, a 16-year-old high school sophomore (Gray, 2018). The petition called for students to walk out of their schools on April 20, the anniversary of the Columbine shooting, which—until Parkland—had been the deadliest high school shooting in U.S. history (Murdock, 2018). By the time of the walkout on April 20, more than 250,000 people had signed the petition and more than 2,000 groups had registered local protests. On the day of the protest, hundreds of thousands of students participated, led primarily by local student groups who individually organized their schools using information and resources offered by the National School Walkout organization.

Throughout the months of March and April, hundreds of thousands of students and their allies engaged in civic protest against gun violence and its impacts on schools. Other than the #ENOUGH National School Walkouts planned by the Women's March, which was itself a grassroots movement that grew out of a politically charged event, these protests were driven and planned by the students themselves. Leveraging social media and the media spotlight placed on them by the Parkland shooting, the student organizers of these protests were able to coordinate a massive social movement whose impacts are still reverberating through our political climate—much like their teachers and the statewide activism they directed against systemic underinvestments in education.

THE TEACHER STRIKES OF THE SPRING OF 2018

Even as hundreds of thousands of students were protesting gun violence, teachers across the country were also engaged in civic activism of their own. Teachers in four different states went on strike in the spring of 2018, and two other states—while avoiding large-scale teacher strikes—experienced widespread teacher demonstrations (see Figure 1.1 for a timeline of student and teacher civic activism in the spring of 2018). These teachers were not motivated by a single incident or policy issue, like students and the Parkland shooting. Instead, they were motivated by a variety of highly interconnected local issues.

The first statewide teacher activism involved over 20,000 teachers across the state of West Virginia. At the time of the strikes in February 2018, West Virginia's average teacher salary was the second lowest in the country at $45,642 (National Education Association [NEA], 2018). West Virginia's teachers had not received a statewide salary increase since 2014. Additionally, due to structural changes to the state's health insurance system, the costs of teachers' health insurance were set to nearly double in July of 2018. Because of these factors, beginning on February 22, teachers in West Virginia went on strike to demand pay increases for teachers and school employees and to prevent increases in the costs of their state-run health insurance system (Wong, 2018). The West Virginia strike led to a complete shutdown of the state's schools (Bidgood, 2018). After nearly 2 weeks of school closures and sustained demonstrations, the strike came to a close when West Virginia's governor signed a bill giving teachers and school staff a 5% pay increase. However, while the statewide increase for school employees ended the 2018 strike, that was not the end of teachers protesting in West Virginia. Almost exactly a year later, in February 2019, over 19,000 teachers went on strike in West Virginia—again closing the majority of schools throughout the state—to protest a state bill that would have allowed for the creation of the first charter schools in the state (Campbell, 2019).

Following closely on the heels of West Virginia's teacher strikes, the next teacher strikes occurred on April 2. In Kentucky, in response to a bill passed by the legislature that sought to privatize and reduce teacher pensions, teachers across the state staged a sick-out on the Friday before spring break and then rallied at the state capitol the next Monday (Blackford, 2018). While many schools were closed for the week due to spring break, many more were forced to close on Friday and Monday. Even with these protests, teachers in Kentucky were unsuccessful in preventing the governor from signing the bill into law a week later on April 10. However, a few days later, on April 14, following sustained pressure from Kentucky's teachers, the Kentucky Legislature successfully voted to override the governor's veto of the 2-year state budget that included a $480 million tax increase and increased funding for public education (Associated Press, 2018a).

Like their colleagues in Kentucky, teachers in Oklahoma also began protesting on April 2, beginning a 9-day statewide teacher strike. Begun by rank-and-file teachers on social media and later endorsed and supported by the Oklahoma Education Association, teachers in Oklahoma, like their peers in West Virginia, were protesting low teacher pay. Additionally, they

Figure 1.1. Timeline of student and teacher civic activism in the spring of 2018.

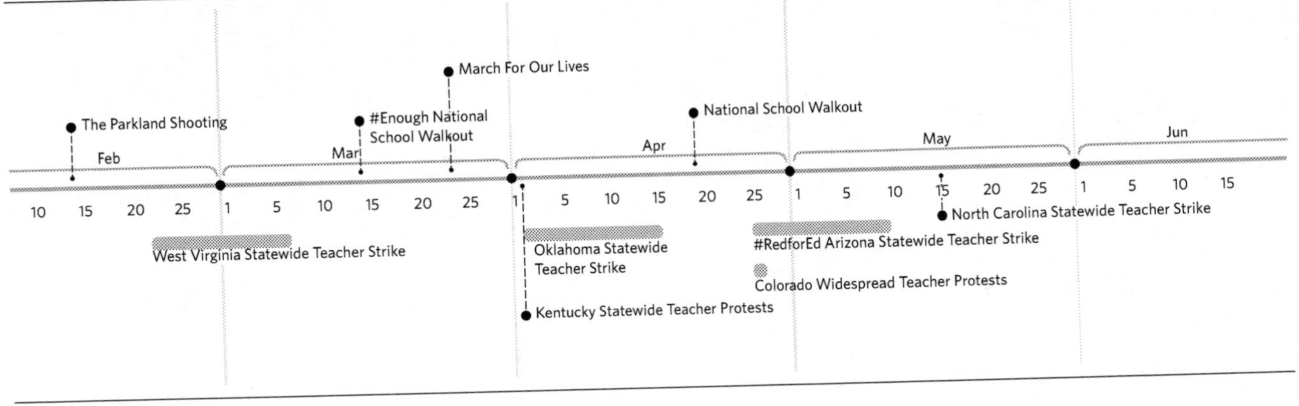
March For Our Lives
The Parkland Shooting
#Enough National School Walkout
National School Walkout
Feb
Mar
Apr
May
Jun
10 15 20 25 1 5 10 15 20 25 1 5 10 15 20 25 1 5 10 15 20 25 1 5 10 15
North Carolina Statewide Teacher Strike
West Virginia Statewide Teacher Strike
Oklahoma Statewide Teacher Strike
#RedforEd Arizona Statewide Teacher Strike
Colorado Widespread Teacher Protests
Kentucky Statewide Teacher Protests

were protesting a general underinvestment in education spending in the state (Goldstein & Dias, 2018). In 2017, Oklahoma ranked third to last in average teacher salary and 47th in the country in per-student revenue (NEA, 2018). Of particular importance to the teachers, Oklahoma's per-pupil education funding had been reduced by 28% since 2008, causing many schools to cut programs and limit the school week to 4 days (DenHoed, 2018). Ultimately, through their protests, Oklahoma teachers were able to secure additional salaries for teachers and support staff as well as additional revenues for schools through tax increases (Goldstein & Dias, 2018).

Next up in the wave of teacher strikes were Arizona and Colorado. In Arizona, an advocacy group called Arizona Educators United, which was independent of Arizona's teacher unions and was organized largely through social media, began staging "walk-ins" on April 11, 2018. These walk-ins involved teachers meeting outside of school and walking into school together at the beginning of the school day in a show of solidarity. Like their colleagues in Oklahoma, Arizona's teachers were seeking increased salaries and greater school funding (Kuhn, 2018). Arizona's average teacher salary was $47,403 in 2016–2017, which was $11,000 less than the national average. Additionally, Arizona had cut taxes every year except one since 1990, resulting in disinvestments from public schools and stagnant teacher salaries (Turner et al., 2018). Indeed, average teacher salaries in Arizona were $8,000–9,000 less than they had been in 1990, and school funding had been reduced by 14% from its 2008 levels. In light of these statistics and following the state's refusal to meet Arizona Educators United's demands, Arizona's teachers engaged in a strike, endorsed by the state's teacher union, beginning on April 26, 2018. This strike led to the closure of over 1,000 schools in the state, affecting approximately three quarters of Arizona's 1.1 million school children (Cano et al., 2018). Ultimately, Arizona's strike ended on May 3, with Arizona's governor signing legislation that would lead to a 20% pay increase for teachers over 3 years (Snow & Tang, 2018).

Colorado's teacher activism, while not as widespread as those in Arizona, was also aimed at low teacher pay and underinvestment in education. Throughout the state, teachers protested throughout April and early May, with the largest protests occurring on April 26 and 27 when upward of 10,000 teachers protested at the state capitol (Hutchinson, 2018). These teachers were protesting an average teacher salary that was over 20% lower than the national average and school funding that had failed to keep pace with inflation or return to pre-2008 levels (Turner et al., 2018). Following the teacher demonstrations, Colorado enacted a state budget that increased K–12 education spending by $150 million. However, due to teacher salaries being set at the local level in Colorado, teachers were unable to achieve a statewide teacher salary increase (Associated Press, 2018b).

The final teacher activism of the spring of 2018 was a 1-day statewide teacher strike in North Carolina on May 16, 2018. Like many of their colleagues, the 20,000 teachers who engaged in this strike were protesting low teacher pay and systemic disinvestment in education (Elk, 2018). North Carolina ranked 44th in average teacher pay in 2017 and the state's education funding had declined by 8% since 2008, ranking North Carolina 43rd in the nation (NEA, 2018). Organized by the North Carolina Association of Educators, the 1-day strike resulted in the closure of schools in 40 school districts and impacted over 1 million students.

These teacher strikes and protests involved thousands of teachers and affected millions of students. While each was motivated by local concerns, they were all reactions to systemic under- and disinvestments in education, whether it was low teacher compensation or inadequate per-pupil expenditures. Many of these protests leveraged existing civic organizations, like teacher unions, though many also developed independent of existing political structures through social media and were only later aligned with existing organizations. Ultimately, each of these strikes informed the others and these teachers, acting together, were largely successful in challenging the status quo in their states. The fact that they occurred in conjunction with widespread student protests indicates a potential sea change in contemporary student and teacher civic activism that warrants further analysis.

Indeed, the student protests and teacher strikes did not just happen simultaneously. Throughout the 2018 student protests and teacher strikes, students and teachers supported each other's activities. Many of the student protests were facilitated by sympathetic teachers and administrators who empowered their students to engage in civic activism. These school personnel supported students in planning and organizing their protests and sought ways to act within contemporary educational policy to facilitate their activities. For example, many school administrators chose to withhold punishment for students who walked out of school, modified class schedules to accommodate protests, or even joined students in their demonstrations. Students, too, supported their teachers during their strikes and demonstrations. Students throughout these states joined their teachers in demonstrating against low teacher pay and underinvestment in education. Finally, student support for their teachers was often instrumental in cultivating public sympathy for the teacher's strikes. Like student and teacher civic activism throughout American history, the student protests and teacher strikes of 2018 have deep connections that show the interrelationship between student and teacher civic activism.

HISTORICAL CONTEXT OF STUDENT AND TEACHER ACTIVISM

The student and teacher civic activism of the spring of 2018 was the latest in a long tradition of such activism in the United States that dates back to the nation's first schools. During the colonial and revolutionary war era, college and university students protested against their schools, applying the lessons of the Revolutionary War to challenge their schools' policies (Noll, 2007). Later, in the mid- to late 1800s, when the common school movement significantly increased the number of public schools in the United States, students continued to protest their schools—though perhaps in less revolutionary ways. These students drew on the civic protest strategies prevalent at the time, namely those of civic movements and organized labor, and were understood within these traditions. This tradition of student protests continued into the tumultuous 1960s and 1970s, perhaps the most famous era of student protests, and, with the Parkland protests of 2018, it continues today. Importantly, throughout this history, students have often been inspired by and protested alongside—and sometimes even on behalf of—their teachers.

Like students, teachers also have a strong history of civic activism in the United States. Often responding to pressing political concerns or issues of organized labor, teacher strikes have been a staple of American political life since at least the 1960s. Within this tradition, teachers have often been influenced by their students and have protested alongside them to achieve shared aims. Throughout the early and mid-1900s, teacher unions and other professional organizations often found their genesis in student-initiated protests—even as these groups in turn promoted students' activism. Later, in the 1960s and '70s, students and teachers often worked together to protest large-scale societal issues, like segregation and the Vietnam War. During this era, they each drew strength and support from each other even as they pursued their own unique goals, namely expressive and privacy rights for students and stronger labor unions for teachers. The student and teacher activism of spring 2018 continued these complicated shared traditions.

This history of student and teacher civic activism aligns with a tradition in America of viewing civic education as one of the fundamental purposes of public schooling. In many ways, America's public schools were founded on the idea that schools should prepare students for civic participation in our democracy. From the time of the Founding Fathers, public figures have argued that the demands of citizenship in a representative democracy require an education intended to prepare students for that purpose (Brown, 1996). In 1779, Thomas Jefferson introduced a "Bill for the More General Diffusion of Knowledge," which—if it had been enacted—would have established a system of publicly funded schools throughout Virginia in order to meet the needs of a democratic form of government. Following the Revolutionary War, other important political figures also explicitly connected education and preparation for citizenship. Benjamin Rush, who signed the Declaration of Independence, advocated for public education to transform young men into "republican machines" who would put the common good above their own self-interests (Rudolph, 1965). Then, in the mid-1800s, during the proliferation of public common schools, common school advocates argued that common public schools were necessary to inculcate national values, including the republican ideology of the new nation. These reformers reasoned that the responsibilities and knowledge necessary for democratic citizenship and popular self-governance necessitated universal public schools (Meyer et al., 1979). These same arguments would be picked up by the nation's courts in the 1900s as they ended segregation in schools and expanded students' rights, due in large part to the important connections between education and citizenship. Given that civic protest is a long-recognized form of civic engagement, the actions of these students and teachers throughout American history align with this historic goal of education in the United States.

THE POLITICAL CONTEXT OF STUDENT AND TEACHER ACTIVISM

While the students and teachers who participated in the spring 2018 protests and strikes continued a long tradition of student and teacher activism that aligns with the civic aims of education, these activities occurred within a unique contemporary political context. Since at least the Industrial Revolution and the common school movement of the mid- to late 1800s, American education has privileged the values of efficiency and control, often modeling schools around the ideal of the factory. Contemporary educational policy continues this emphasis on efficiency and control, but, since at least 1983, educational policy in the United States has been dominated by a loose coalition of conservative ideologies that prioritize the connection between education and the economy while downplaying education's role in civic development (Apple, 2005, 2006). Exemplified by *A Nation at Risk*, the 1983 federal report that argued the state of America's schools threatened the nation's economic and political dominance, this coalition of ideologies has fostered a policy paradigm that has reshaped the landscape of educational policy (Mehta, 2013). Policy paradigms are the master narratives or ideological frameworks through which we understand and make sense of complex realities (Hall, 1993; Kuhn, 1962). They shape both politics (Baumgartner & Jones, 1993; Mehta, 2013) and the cognitive maps of how we think about an issue, including what we identify as policy problems, how we define those problems, and the range of potential or desirable solutions for those problems (Hall, 1993; Legro, 2000). As such, policy paradigms, like the A Nation at Risk paradigm, profoundly impact policies and practice.

Since 1983, education policy in the United States has come to be dominated by the A Nation at Risk paradigm, where educational policy has been characterized by the centralization of educational policy decisions, the injection of market logic into educational policy, and tighter systems of control over schools, teachers, and students. Together, these shifts have reshaped the purpose of education, what it means to be educated, and the definition of citizenship and civic agency. The A Nation at Risk paradigm fosters a version of citizenship that conflates democracy with capitalism and active citizenship with passive consumerism (Mirra & Morrell, 2011). Within this context, student and teacher civic agency has come to be redefined in ways that limit the political power and voice of these groups while simultaneously positioning them as passive recipients of educational policy decisions. Thus, while American schools have often been controlling and totalitarian institutions, educational policy since 1983 marks a shift in both the goals for education and how schools, teachers, and students have come to be understood and positioned within educational policy.

Yet, despite these shifts in educational policy, more than 35 years into this policy paradigm, students and teachers rocked the nation in 2018 by engaging in the largest school-based civic activism since the 1960s. By continuing long, interconnected histories of student and teacher activism that align with ideas about the democratic purposes of education, these activities constitute a rejection of the A Nation at Risk paradigm, both in its policy outcomes and in the way it redefines and constrains student and teacher civic agency. As such, student and teacher protests provide a natural foundation from which to theorize—and realize—an alternative to the A Nation at Risk paradigm.

ORGANIZATION OF THE BOOK

To contextualize contemporary student and teacher protests, the second and third chapters explore the history of student and teacher activism, looking at how these activities align with historic understandings of the civic purposes of education. These chapters situate these activities within a historical framework that shows the long tradition of these practices, their deep connections, and the ways in which they have impacted and been understood within larger social movements throughout American history. Only through understanding the ways in which larger societal forces have both shaped and been shaped by student and teacher activism can we understand the full impact of the A Nation at Risk paradigm on student and teacher agency and the ways in which these activities challenge and interrupt that paradigm.

The fourth chapter more fully explores the A Nation at Risk paradigm. It focuses on the theoretical understandings of its underlying ideologies and the ways in which they have found expression in practice and policy in and around schools. With a firm understanding of the A Nation at Risk paradigm, this chapter then addresses the ways in which these forces have impacted and shaped student and teacher agency. The chapter explores both theoretical understandings of civic agency as well as the tensions between the paradigm's conception of civic agency and other conceptions of civic agency not endorsed or recognized within the paradigm. The chapter concludes with a discussion of the ways in which student and teacher civic agency is limited in practice, including in the legal protections for student and teacher activism.

Chapter 5 combines the lessons of the earlier chapters to explore the events of 2018 in the context of both the history of student and teacher civic activism and the A Nation at Risk paradigm. On the one hand, the 2018 protests continue a long tradition of student and teacher activism. On the other, the A Nation at Risk paradigm has largely redefined teacher and student civic agency in ways that are inconsistent with these protests and strikes; from within the paradigm, students and teachers are understood as the passive recipients of policy, not participants in its creation. Student protests and teacher strikes occurred at the intersection of these two historical and ideological traditions. Navigating these tensions will help us understand how these activities came to be, how they relate to both these traditions, and the potential implications they hold for the future.

Chapter 6 then offers a discussion of what educational policy might look like if school leaders and policymakers embrace and seriously grapple with student and teacher agency as an alternative to the A Nation at Risk paradigm. This chapter begins by theorizing an educational policy paradigm, an Education for Citizenship paradigm, with its foundations in the lived experiences of student and teacher civic activism. With this theoretical understanding, the chapter continues with a discussion of the ideological shifts necessary to realize this alternate educational policy paradigm. In discussing these paradigmatic shifts, the chapter applies these shifts to the challenges and promise of student and teacher civic agency to assist policymakers and educational leaders in beginning to implement policies and practices that embrace teacher and student agency, while balancing other valid concerns.

Finally, chapter 7 investigates contemporary education policy and student and teacher civic activism since the spring of 2018, as well as political responses to these activities, to explore how policymakers and educational leaders have navigated the tensions between the A Nation at Risk paradigm and student and teacher civic agency. Since the spring of 2018, teachers have continued to strike both at the local and state level, in pursuit of traditional labor rights and in pursuit of systemic policy changes and increased school funding. Students, too, have continued to protest, including international youth-led climate protests and civil rights protests that align with the Black Lives Matter movement. Through exploring the persistent phenomenon of student and teacher civic activism and the political responses to these activities, this chapter demonstrates the continuing tension between the A Nation at Risk paradigm and the ideologies that inform an Education for Citizenship paradigm. While these tensions demonstrate the continued strength of the A Nation at Risk paradigm and the ways in which it shapes our collective understandings of education, this conflict potentially foreshadows future fault lines in education policy—especially around issues of civics education.

Ultimately, exploring the deep and interconnected history of student and teacher activism as well as the A Nation at Risk paradigm and its impact on student and teacher civic agency will allow us to more fully situate these protests in their political context. Only then can we understand how these activities offer an alternative to the A Nation at Risk paradigm that is grounded in student and teacher civic agency.

CHAPTER 2

History of Student Protests in the United States

The student and teacher civic activism during the spring of 2018 was the latest in a long tradition in American education. Throughout American history, students and teachers have demonstrated at and against their schools to challenge perceived societal wrongs. These activities have been understood within their social and political contexts as continuations of contemporaneous civic activism. Importantly, though, these activities also affected and even propelled wider societal movements. The history of student and teacher civic activism demonstrates the strong tradition of these activities, their deep connections, and their place within larger social movements. Ultimately, this history shows that student and teacher civic activism is an important aspect of the history of education in the United States—one that aligns with a dominant historical and philosophical justification for public education in America, the idea that education ought to prepare individuals for democratic citizenship. The history of student and teacher activism stands in stark contrast to the dominant ideologies and policy prescriptions of the contemporary A Nation at Risk paradigm.

Primary and secondary students in the United States have been protesting for nearly as long as they have been attending formal schools. From the earliest reported strike of primary students at a parochial school in Brooklyn in 1886 to the national string of protests in response to the Parkland shooting in 2018, K–12 students have consistently exercised their collective agency by protesting at and against their schools. Since America's founding, these protests have taken many forms and have been in response to a vast array of policy decisions and political issues. Some students have walked out of their schools, others have gone on strike, and still others have staged sit-ins, engaged in petition writing and write-in campaigns, and acted off school grounds entirely to protest larger societal issues. While the protests of college or university students have the longer history and have influenced the growth of later protests in K–12 settings, K–12 students have their own robust history of civic protests.

Spanning over a century, what these protests have in common is not their means or their ends but their purpose. Each protest was in response to a matter of pressing concern to the students involved. They sought to correct perceived injustices by banding together, amplifying their voices, and forcing decision-makers to take heed. Ultimately, these student protests have taken many forms, been met with a variety of responses, and have had mixed success. The earliest protests were met with patronizing good humor. However, once these protests began to spread and influence school decision-makers, they become a matter of serious concern to parents, school officials, and the larger community. Since then, student protests have been the source of both praise and condemnation. Often, these protests were praised as students exercising the very democratic virtues and traits whose cultivation motivated public education in the United States. On the other hand, these activities were often condemned because these students challenged the status quo and were viewed as illegitimate participants in civic dialogue. They were seen as too young, too inexperienced, or too naïve to be productive participants in society's larger democratic conversations.

The discussion that follows demonstrates how, throughout American history, K–12 students have engaged in organized civic protests. They have protested in many ways and for a variety of causes. They have proven that their voices matter and that their perspectives are important, though they are often absent or excluded from larger social conversations. These students have also demonstrated that they are attuned to and influenced by larger social issues, often adopting the causes and methods of their elders, especially college students. While student protesters were often influenced by the methods of other groups and sometimes adopted their goals, students have also offered unique perspectives and approaches to issues that were deeply important to them that inspired others in turn. Indeed, in some cases, these student protests have led the way both in methods and substance, giving rise to larger social movements, protests, and ultimately societal change.

EARLY STUDENT PROTESTS FROM THE REVOLUTIONARY WAR THROUGH THE LATE 1800s

Prior to the mid-1800s, most formal schooling in the United States was done in small private institutions, religious institutions, or the home. What formal education that did exist at the time occurred at private and religious colleges and universities. As such, these were the first sites of student protests in the United States, with protests dating back to the founding of these institutions. Indeed, prior to Harvard College's (now Harvard University) first commencement in 1642, two "exorbitant children . . . raised a riot" (Novak, 1977, p. 1). While this may have been the first recorded instance of student protest in the United States, college and university students did not engage in widespread protests until the period around the Revolutionary War. These protests coincided with a general democratization that occurred in American society. While these protests were often viewed as jovial affairs—one Harvard protest about the quality of the school's food involved student demands for school officials to "behold our Butter stinketh . . . give us, we pray thee, Butter that stinketh not" (Novak, 1977, p. 5)—they were largely accepted by society and school officials as extensions of revolutionary ideologies. As one paper at the time put it when discussing student protests, "How happy ought we to esteem ourselves when we see some of our youth who will probably fill some of the highest stations in their country when their fathers have fallen asleep, so early declaring their love to their country" (Novak, 1977, p. 4). In the mind of people of the time, student protests were patriotic and embodied laudable democratic values.

In addition to being viewed in light of revolutionary and democratic ideals, college and university students at the time also adopted revolutionary methods in their protests. Students hung effigies of public figures, burned goods taxed by the British, and delivered speeches on liberty and democracy. They also engaged in more radical methods. At Princeton in 1802, the main hall suffered a mysterious fire during students' midday meal. Reverend Samuel Smith, the current university president, deemed it arson "committed by design, presumably by firebrands tainted by the radical principles of Jeffersonian democracy" (Noll, 2007, p. 96). Similarly, Harvard experienced a revolt in 1807, called the Rotten Cabbage Rebellion, in which students protested unfair discipline and the deplorable state of the food in the college commons. As part of the pattern of unrest that gripped Harvard during this time, students raided the chapel, broke a window, threw furniture onto the lawn, and set it ablaze, among other instances of general disruption and insubordination (Novak, 1977).

During the period following the Revolutionary War until the late 1800s, college and university students' protests were generally local in scope and limited in duration. These students were primarily protesting in opposition to their university's leadership or against draconian *in loco parentis* rules that sought to severely limit what was acceptable behavior (Brax, 1981). One illustrative example during this time took place at the University of California, Berkeley. Attempting to oust an unpopular university president from his position, students crashed a ladder through a window of the president's house and caused other disruptions across the campus.

While most student protests at this time were aimed at local matters, abolition and antislavery student groups were a notable exception. These student groups often clashed with school administrators as they pursued their goals, which included agitating for abolition and smuggling runaway slaves north to Canada. Amherst College in Massachusetts experienced one such group, the Auxiliary Anti-Slavery Society, which at its peak counted one fourth of the student population as members, before the university's president ordered the group to disband in 1834 (Brax, 1981). Ultimately, this history demonstrates that college and university students in America have a long tradition of protesting against their schools—one that primary and secondary students would take up beginning in the late 1800s during the common school movement in the United States.

A BURLESQUE ON STRIKES: THE FIRST REPORTED PRIMARY AND SECONDARY STUDENT PROTESTS, 1886

Like their university peers, once there were primary and secondary common schools in the United States against which to protest, primary and secondary students also engaged in civic activism. The Industrial Revolution and the activities of common school reformers like Horace Mann in the years between 1830 and 1860 quickly grew the nation's loose collection of educational institutions into a vast network of public schools that served a much greater portion of the country's population, including a burgeoning system of primary schools. Consequently, access to education and the quantity of education available to students greatly increased during this time. Fishlow (1966) estimates that in 1800 the average American received a total of 210 days of schooling in their lifetime; in 1850, that number had doubled, and in 1900, the average American was receiving approximately 1,050 days of formal schooling. With these incredible increases in both the number of students and in the time students spent at school, it is little wonder that schools came to be targets of primary and secondary students' ire and protest.

Early student protests were often local in scope and directed against the students' schools in response to the decisions of local school officials. The students of these early protests were attempting to correct local and often personal injustices. These protests were often against decisions such as the firing of a beloved teacher, the hiring of a hated principal, a proposal to extend the school day, the cancelling of a school dance, or the tyrannical takeover of the schools by a hostile school board. While the motivations for these protests were local and the protests themselves were often directed against the school and school officials, the methods employed by these students echoed those used by adults at the time. These protests were understood within—and as extensions of—larger traditions of the time, such as organized labor and civic agitation.

The earliest widely circulated report of a K–12 student protest in the United States appeared in *The New York Times* on March 18, 1886 (see Figure 2.1). Under the headline "A Burlesque on Strikes. Pupils of a Parochial School in Brooklyn Catch the Contagion," the story outlines how a group of students orchestrated a strike of St. Anne's Parochial School in Brooklyn. As the title makes clear, the author of this piece viewed the student's strike as an absurd or comical imitation of contemporary labor strikes. At the time, the school was charging its pupils a fee of 10 cents per week. The article explains how some students, out of a sense of "duty to

Figure 2.1. "A Burlesque on Strikes."

A BURLESQUE ON STRIKES.

PUPILS OF A PAROCHIAL SCHOOL IN BROOKLYN CATCH THE CONTAGION.

The most remarkable strike that has yet grown out of a difference of opinion between the person or persons fixing wages or making rules and those for whom wages are fixed or rules made occurred in Brooklyn the other day. And not the least remarkable feature of this singular affair was the fact that a detective actually discovered its existence and put an end to it. This detective is attached to the Second Police Precinct, and has a son who is one of the pupils of St. Anne's Parochial School. One day last week the father noticed that, although the hour was past school time, his boy apparently had no intention of quitting the house. Inquiry into the matter brought from the son the statement that it would be useless for him to start for school, as he would not be permitted to enter. The father's first thought was of course that the boy had been sent home in disgrace, for some act of insubordination or misbehavior, and that consequently the rattan might have to be introduced into the discussion. Further inquiry, however, dispelled this unpleasant impression. The boy said the pupils had gone on strike, and with the boy's aptitude at imitating his elders, had organized and proposed to fight.

Upon hearing this startling statement the detective sprang up in a hurry and told his son to prepare at once for school. He sent the boy on in advance and followed after in citizen's clothes, keeping behind far enough to appear to have no interest in the boy and yet near enough to afford him instant protection. Upon approaching the school building, sure enough, three boys, who had been appointed a committee by the strikers, were discovered on picket duty. Perceiving that an attempt was about to be made by a pupil to enter the school building in defiance of the strikers, two of the committeemen ran forward to assault the "scab." But the detective was too quick for them. Probably two boys were never quite so surprised and taken aback since boys were first invented as were these committeemen when they found themselves taken by their collars and irresistibly impelled into school. This summary and tyrannical proceeding broke up the strike by depriving it of its most determined leaders, raising the blockade and giving the " scabs" a chance to return to their books.

Such of the pupils in attendance at St. Anne's school as are able to do so are required to pay each a weekly fee of 10 cents. Some boy of an economical turn of mind bruited about among his companions, and converted them to it, the opinion that this charge was exorbitant, and that their duty to their parents required them to have It cut down 50 per cent. But, with a spirit of equity not always discovered among persons intent on redressing wrongs, since they had decided to cut down the school's revenues one-half, they magnanimously offered to relieve the school of half its work. In other words, they expressed an entire willingness to cut the school days down to three a week. It was because the school authorities declined to accept the new schedule that the reformers struck and took steps to keep the "scabs" away. The strikers were not punished, the humor of the affair being so thoroughly appreciated as to save them.

Note. First published in *The New York Times* on March 18, 1886.

their parents," sought to reduce the fee to 5 cents per week while also of-fering "to relieve the school of half its work" by reducing the school week down to 3 days. The school (for some reason) refused the boys' offer, and in response the boys instigated a strike of the school, complete with a "picket" line to prevent "scabs"—a contemporary term for someone who engages in work during a strike—from entering the school.

The perspective of the article's author on the protest is clear; they find the notion of a students' strike quite humorous. The title of the article, "A Burlesque on Strikes," indicates that the author viewed the students' actions as a parody or a caricature of the actions of organized labor of the time.

While the article suggests that this early student protest was not to be taken seriously, the protest itself captured the imagination of both other students and the country. Ten days after the article appeared in *The New York Times*, it was reprinted in its entirety in the *Chicago Daily Tribune* ("A Burlesque on Strikes," 1886). A few weeks later, on the front page, *The Boston Globe* reported a story titled "School Boys on a Strike" (1886) that described the actions of a group of students, again in Brooklyn, this time at Public School 34, who went on strike to demand a half-hour recess every afternoon and a half holiday on Fridays. *The Globe* article, while it retains some of *The New York Times*' article's levity, does not frame these strikes as humorous parodies of adult activity. Instead, its language suggests that the author viewed these strikes as a serious matter. The article frames the stu-dents' protest as a serious breach of the peace and the protesters as violent delinquents. Gone was the flippant, indulgent language of *The New York Times* article. Instead, the students engaged in this protest were portrayed as violent threats to order and propriety.

On April 21, 1886, one week after *The Globe* article reported on contin-ued student protests in Brooklyn, *The Atlanta Journal-Constitution*—again on the front page—reported on a student walkout in Boston. Continuing the shift away from viewing these protests as the humorous antics of chil-dren, the article described how 60 pupils of the South Boston public school marched around the city with painted banners and then picketed outside their school before being dispersed by police. The article itself is clinical and impersonal in its description of the protest, but the article appears below the headline "The Modern Schoolboy" (1886). The title, by associating the protests with the modern schoolboy and by extension a lack of protests with the schoolboys of the past, seems to lament this new development. *The Atlanta Journal-Constitution* article perhaps best demonstrates the shift in understanding of this new phenomenon of student protests. Rather than be-ing subjects of ridicule or humor, these new protests became the subject of serious reporting and began to elicit strong, often negative, reactions.

Not all of the reporting on these emerging student protests was nega-tive, however. On June 1, 1886, the *Chicago Daily Tribune* published a news article about a successful student protest in Lancaster, Wisconsin

("Wisconsin: Pupils Strike for a Holiday and Get It," 1886). The students petitioned their principal to dismiss school in order to observe Decoration Day, an early precursor to Memorial Day, in honor of those who died during the Civil War. After the principal rejected the students' initial request, the students wrote and circulated a petition and delivered it to the school board, who ultimately granted the holiday and closed the school. This is the first reported incident where the primary student protestors were successful in achieving their aims.

In addition to demonstrating how student protests came to be a matter of serious public concern, the news articles of 1886 also foreshadow three important themes of student protests in the United States. First, the students in these articles adopted the methods of other political groups of the time and were understood within these larger traditions. The "A Burlesque on Strikes" article that appeared in both *The New York Times* and the *Chicago Daily Tribune* uses language that explicitly connects the student protests to organized labor protests. It calls these students' actions a "strike" and speaks of the pupils "catch[ing] the contagion" of striking and "imitating [their] elders" ("A Burlesque on Strikes," 1886, p. 8). The article also mentions the boys forming a picket line to prevent "scabs" from entering the school. Thus, not only was this protest understood within the tradition of labor protests of the time, it was also clearly motivated by them at least in regards to the students' chosen methods. The "School Boys on Strike" article from *The Boston Globe* makes this connection even more explicitly. The article stated that "[t]he principal and teachers have always advised the pupils to read the newspapers, and the success of recent labor movements left a strong impression on their minds" ("School Boys on Strike," 1886, p. 1). Even in these earliest protests, students were learning from their elders and using this knowledge to inform their actions.

Second, these articles demonstrate that, while students adopted the strategies of other groups, they were often motivated by local circumstances or the decisions of local authorities that directly and intimately impacted them. The students at issue in the 1886 articles were not protesting larger societal inequalities or state or national policies. They were protesting local decisions and local policies. The sights of protest were almost exclusively a single school, and the subjects of the protest were typically a single decision or failure to act on behalf of school personnel.

Third, as demonstrated even within these few news articles, it is clear that reactions to student protests have been—and continue to be—mixed. The first article from *The New York Times* seems to demean the students even as it expresses awe at their gumption. *The Boston Globe* article seems to swing the other direction, painting the protesting students in a negative light as violent and destructive. Similarly, *The Atlanta Journal-Constitution* also embraces a negative view of the "modern schoolboy," implicitly comparing these students to the idealized students of the past. And yet, even in this time, where many thought that these striking students were deviants and a threat to public order, there were those who seemed to embrace and celebrate what these students were doing. The *Chicago Daily Tribune* article that reported on the students' successful protest to compel the school to observe Decoration Day seems to bask in the notion that these students were able to convince their principal to observe the holiday. Admittedly, this tacit approval may be due to the content of the protest—observing a holiday honoring those who died in the Civil War—but, even if this is the case, it is equally important that the venue and participants in the protest did not override whatever support the article's author felt toward the goals of the protest.

These mixed reactions to student protests in 1886 can be partly explained by conflicting understandings of schools and the purposes of education at the time, which differed on whether schools should foster democratic citizenship and participation among students or ready them to participate in the newly industrialized economy. After the American Revolution, one of the principal arguments for schooling was to promote republican ideology and the traits and dispositions of democratic citizenship. Thomas Jefferson, the principal author of the Declaration of Independence, expressed the idea that "education is necessary to prepare citizens to participate effectively and intelligently in our open political system if we are to preserve freedom and independence" (as quoted in *Wisconsin v. Yoder*, 1972, p. 221). Building from Jefferson and the educational thinking of the Founding Fathers, education for democratic citizenship was one of the founding justifications for the common school movement of the mid-1800s that gave rise to America's public school system (Meyer et al., 1979). Horace Mann (1849), one of the key figures of the common school movement, argued:

[U]nder our republican government, it seems clear that the minimum of this education can never be less than such as sufficient to qualify each citizen for the civil and social duties he will be called to discharge, such an education as is indispensable for the civil functions of a witness or a juror; as is necessary for the voter in municipal and in national affairs; and finally, as is requisite for the faithful and conscientious discharge of all those duties which devolve upon the inheritor of a portion of the sovereignty of this great republic. (p. 17)

Proponents of common schools, relying in part on arguments based on the democratic outcomes of public education like those expressed by Mann, were successful in developing public school systems across the country.

Additionally, during the 19th century, the Industrial Revolution had gripped America. Factories came to dominate the urban labor market and skilled trades were replaced with machines and those who operated them. This transition to a factory system was so pronounced that, between the years of 1860 and 1900, the value of manufactured goods in the United

States increased eightfold (Brownlee, 1979). The quick industrialization of America had profound impacts on its emerging schools. More children attended more schools for longer, and the schools themselves were influenced by the idea of the factory, which had so captured America's imagination. During this "age of the factory," schools took on the characteristics of the factory and aligned themselves both with its ideologies and goals. This influenced not only the structure and organization of schools but also their character and goals. Schooling at the time focused on instilling the values of the factory such as industriousness and responsibility, while also teaching basic literacy, numbers, and other traditional subjects. These schools were intentionally bent toward preparing students for the emerging industrial order, one marked by status distinctions between workers and owners as well as a drive for efficiency (Nasaw, 1979).

With the dual social understandings that schools ought to both promote and attain efficiency and that students ought to learn both civic and industrial habits, it is easy to see how these protests could elicit a wide array of reactions. On the one hand, these students were demonstrating and practicing the very traits of democratic citizenship upon which the common school movement had been founded. On the other hand, these students were disrupting the efficiency of the system and were often seen as illegitimate participants in school governance and democratic discourse.

As these early examples demonstrate, like other forms of political protests, student protests have been met with conflicting reactions but, unlike other protests, these reactions have often been complicated by the age of the participants and societal perceptions of schools as inappropriate venues for protest. But these conflicting reactions did not stem the rising tide of student protests across the country. In fact, in the years between 1886 and 1950, over 2,000 primary and secondary student protests were reported throughout the United States. These protests were largely local in nature and scope, but toward the mid-1930s, 1940s, and early 1950s, students—especially the growing ranks of high school students—began taking a broader view.

A NATIONAL TREND OF LOCAL PROTESTS: STUDENT PROTESTS FROM 1886–1934

Following the student strikes of 1886, hundreds of protests swept America's primary and secondary schools. This was a time of significant growth in America's public school system, especially its high schools. In 1890, approximately 300,000 young adults attended high school (Goldin & Katz, 1999; Herbst, 1996). By 1930, that number had increased to nearly 5 million, or approximately half of the nation's teenagers, an increase of over 1,500%. The increase was so pronounced that a new high school was established nearly every day during this time (Goldin & Katz, 1999). Perhaps not surprisingly, as more and more young people chose—or were compelled through compulsory attendance laws—to pursue secondary education, the proliferation of high schools was met with an even greater increase in student activism at those schools.

The student protests between the 1890s and the mid-1930s were typically limited to a single school or occasionally an entire school district and were often in direct response to the decisions of local school officials. Students during this time were protesting a variety of decisions—both large and small—of school officials that directly impacted them, their experiences with school, and their education. The most common inciting incident for a student protest was the dismissal of a beloved teacher or principal. In one typical example out of Philadelphia in 1887, over 400 students, ages 5 to 15 years old, protested the firing of their principal by the local school board ("A School on Strike," 1887). The board had decided to fire the principal for her insubordinate refusal to administer an examination requested by two of the board members. The students, after hearing of the decision of the board to vacate the principal's position, walked out of school, paraded through the streets holding brooms calling for the board to be "swept clean," and ultimately picketed in front of their school. During the protest, some of the students decorated themselves with badges and began calling themselves the "Knights of McClellan," which was the name of their school, in homage to the Knights of Labor, a labor organization of the time that was responsible for the first mass organization of the working class in the United States.

Perhaps one of the reasons the removal of teachers or principals by school boards was such a contentious issue for so many students of this time was due to the lack of teacher job protections and the nature of teachers' positions. Local teacher unions, while they did exist in some places, were not widespread in the early 1900s. This meant that teachers and principals did not have tenure protections and their employment was often at the whim of elected school boards. Many teachers' positions were appointed yearly and often involved systems of patronage (Heilbron, 1974). Because of this, teachers and principals often found themselves in tenuous positions when new school board members were elected. These new board members were often hostile to existing personnel, viewing them as potentially disloyal, and sought to install their own people into these positions. This often led to teachers and principals being unceremoniously removed from their positions, usually for reasons unrelated to—and often in spite of—their performance, ability, or reputation.

Students during this time weren't always protesting the unjust and politically motivated removal of teachers or principals. Sometimes students were protesting against the decisions of teachers and principals or even agitating for their removal (see, e.g., "Students Were Winners," 1889). These protests were spurred on by a variety of decisions by school personnel. While some of these decisions were seemingly innocuous—like the banning of a particular dance ("School Wants Tango," 1913) or the assignment of difficult math problems as a punishment ("Pasadena Students Get Up In Revolt," 1902)—others fundamentally shifted students' relationships and experiences with their schools. Often at the heart of these protests were decisions to extend the school day or to curtail student organizations and fraternization. In one memorable example, approximately 100 students protested their principal's decision to ban "class parties," an early form of school dances ("Grim Student War Threatens," 1908). The protesting students, dressed in sheets and nightgowns, paraded through their town's main street carrying a coffin that bore the inscription "School Spirit Foully Murdered." In another, more serious example, students in Chicago staged walkouts, strikes, and petition campaigns, and even brought legal challenges in an effort to prevent the school district leadership from banning secret societies—an early form of fraternities and sororities (Pruter, 2003). These societies of students were often in opposition to school officials and had created a cabal that completely controlled the school's athletic programs.

Like the protests of 1886, student protests of this time were influenced by and understood within larger social traditions, especially organized labor and burgeoning civic organizations. Many of these protests were understood as strikes, a term strongly associated with the actions of organized labor, both by the students themselves and outside observers. While it became less common for students to attempt to form picket lines to prevent scabs from entering the school, it's clear that organized labor's activities still informed these students' actions and methods. These students saw themselves as continuing the tradition of organized labor in banding together to oppose concentrated authority.

Similarly, models of civic participation at the time outside of labor also influenced students' methods. Many reports of student protests at the time discuss how students would hold "indignation meetings" prior to initiating any sort of group action (e.g., "Pasadena Students Get Up In Revolt," 1902, p. A7). When students felt aggrieved by a policy or decision, they would hold these indignation meetings to discuss the issue. Any student who wanted to speak on the issue was invited to attend, and adults or authority figures were often excluded. At these meetings, students would share their perspectives and discuss what, if any, action would be taken to address the issue. Outside of student protests, indignation meetings were well understood at the time and were commonly practiced in America when citizens sought to challenge or protest public proceedings (Oxford English Dictionary Online, 2018).

In addition to being influenced by the methods of labor and broader civic participation, students during this time occasionally adopted their goals as well. In one protest in San Francisco in 1917, students walked out and struck against their school due to teachers at the school riding on the local streetcars while the streetcar employees were on strike for higher wages ("Boys Join Strikers," 1917). While directed against the school and the actions of the teachers, these students were protesting out of sympathy toward the streetcar employees. This is perhaps one of the earliest examples of a primary or secondary school protest that, while directed locally toward school employees, touches on and seeks to influence larger societal issues.

The years between 1886 and 1935 were marked by a wave of student protests throughout the country, but for the most part each protest was in response to local issues and addressed to local decision-makers. Thus, even though there were thousands of student protests during this time, it was less a national wildfire of protest and more a national constellation of frequent, and sometimes brilliant, flashes of student unrest. Students during this time sought to address local issues, even as they were influenced by active civic and political groups of the time. But this wasn't only a one-way phenomenon. Student protests also informed and influenced the very labor unions and civic groups that they emulated. In one example, students in Milwaukee staged a walkout and strike of their school in response to the school board's termination of the superintendent ("Teachers May Strike, Too," 1927). Following the student strike, a local community group, the Cudahy Women's Club, was formed to also oppose the actions of the board and support the students. In addition, the protest spurred the high school teachers to band together to protest the school board. They met and voted to join the students' protest. This phenomenon of student activism informing other civic groups is also demonstrated by one of the largest, longest, and perhaps most significant protests of the time. In San Diego in 1918, students staged a 3-month strike of the high school, culminating in two school board members' resignations, three board members losing recall elections, and the formation of the San Diego Teacher Union.

An Exemplar: The San Diego High School Protest of 1918

In 1917, three new candidates were elected to the five-member San Diego School Board (Heilbron, 1974). San Diego at the time was a city of approximately 70,000 and had a single high school. These new board members had run their campaigns on a promise to oppose the reappointment of the superintendent of San Diego's schools, Duncan MacKinnon, who was well respected but had raised some ire by supporting a bond issue to finance a new stadium. After being elected, the three new board members formed a solid majority—to such an extent that the three of them earned the nickname "the solid three"—and began asserting themselves in the operations of the schools.

Toward the end of the 1916–1917 school year, the solid three distributed a survey to the teachers of the school district. Ostensibly, the purpose of the survey was to collect information about the schools and their teaching force. However, due to the lack of job protections for teachers and the political nature of many teaching positions within a loose system of patronage, the teachers interpreted the survey as a threat against the prior administration and an implicit loyalty pledge. One question on the survey asked teachers if they "feel that you can work in harmony with the new management and give them the loyal support necessary for success in school work?" This caused 77 of the 94 faculty members of the high school, after holding their own indignation meeting, to submit a joint reply.

The teachers' concerns proved to be well founded. In November 1917, the solid three passed a resolution that MacKinnon would not be retained by the district. Then, in June 1918, the board dismissed 19 high school teachers and the high school principal, who were viewed as being supportive of MacKinnon. The student body's reaction to the mass firing of nearly a quarter of the high school teaching staff was immediate and forceful. On June 6, the Executive Committee of the Student Body held a massive indignation meeting—ironically held in the stadium that MacKinnon financed—of more than half of the school's 1,500 students. At the meeting, the students discussed the actions of the board and the dismissal of their teachers. Ultimately, the students adopted a resolution against the board's actions:

> Resolved that the student bodies of the San Diego High School and Junior College leave and not return to school until the Board of Education has given satisfactory reasons, other than political, for the dismissal of several teachers, and furthermore, that they offer to reinstate all who are not proved inefficient. (Heilbron, 1974)

After voting to adopt the resolution, the students walked out of their school and marched to deliver the resolution to the members of the board. The next day, June 7, only 12 of the nearly 1,500 students attended school.

Public reactions to the students' strike of the school were mixed. Many community members expressed support of the students, though a few questioned the propriety of the student protest. One letter to the editor eloquently discussed these tensions, writing:

> There are few occasions that could justify or even excuse actions such as those of the students of our high school last Thursday. Commonly, such a manifestation is disruptive of discipline and merely disintegrating and ought, therefore, to be discountenanced by anyone who believes, as I believe, that the idea of order is one of the fundamentals of all government. Now and then, however, there arise circumstances in which persons entrusted with a little brief authority so flagrantly abuse it that it becomes necessary to take such action within the limits of the law as will call the attention of the community to the extent and gravity of the evil. (Heilbron, 1974)

The author of this letter, Charles C. Haines, clearly supported the students' actions even as he questioned the appropriateness of students in general engaging in civic protest. Importantly, though, he understood and positioned these students within larger democratic processes. These students were violating a "fundamental" idea of all governments, but it was acceptable for them to do so since they were doing it to draw public attention to the abuses of democratically elected officials in an attempt to correct those abuses.

The student leaders of the walkout and other concerned community members continued to meet during the students' strike and began to instigate recall proceedings against the board majority. During this time, community members made it clear that they were following the students' lead. The leader of the Citizens' Committee, a citizen group also opposed to the board majority, stated at one meeting that they "would continue the good fight started by the students" (Heilbron, 1974). San Diego teachers also came together to join the students in pursing their goals. The San Diego's Teachers' Association came into being during this time, and its members continued to push the board for its justifications in dismissing the fired teachers. Also of interest, perhaps as an attempt to undermine critiques that they were merely striking to avoid schoolwork, students engaged in community service during the strike. Many volunteered with the Red Cross ("Striking San Diego Students Pass Time Helping Red Cross," 1918). After more than 3 months on strike, the students returned to school at the beginning of the 1918–1919 school year. Then, in December 1918, during the recall election, the solid three were voted out of office by a margin of more than three to one.

The San Diego student protest demonstrates many of the traits of protests at this time. The students were reacting to the local decisions of school authorities that deeply impacted their experiences with school. In many circumstances, this meant seemingly unselfish support for their teachers and administrators in the face of a hostile school board. The San Diego High School students were also acting and understood within a democratic tradition that informed the style and substance of their activism. Perhaps most importantly, though, this protest demonstrates the complicated connection between student protests and other community groups. The actions of the students of San Diego High School were the catalyst for a massive community movement, which was led and informed by students. The students' actions also corresponded with the formation of the San Diego teacher's union. These two phenomena may have grown out of a common incident—the firing of 19 teachers—but the student protests preceded and certainly influenced the teachers as they also organized to consolidate their own political power. These student protestors, then, were not merely imitating their elders; they were leading them.

CONNECTING THE LOCAL, THE NATIONAL, AND THE GLOBAL: THE STUDENT PROTEST MOVEMENTS OF 1935–1974

Prior to 1935, most student protests were motivated by local decisions and directed at local decision-makers. This began to change in 1935 and ultimately reached a zenith in the 1960s and '70s when primary and secondary students—along with their peers in colleges and universities—were engaged in a variety of national movements, protesting on issues of national importance and local impact, like the civil rights movement, the Vietnam War, and the student rights movement.

The first nationwide student movement in the United States occurred in the 1930s, culminating in a nationwide student strike that occurred on April 12, 1935 (Cohen, 1997). Organized by the National Student Strike Committee, a loose collection of college and university students as well as some secondary students, the protest promoted peace and sought to prevent the United States from entering another armed conflict in Europe ("Nation's Students 'Strike' for Peace," 1935). The students planning the protest estimated that 125,000 primary, secondary, and postsecondary students participated across the country in a 1-hour walkout and strike of their schools. The majority of protests occurred at colleges and universities, but many high school students also participated in the mass protest, though the high school protests were less well organized due, in part, to less well-established social activist groups at those schools.

What is remarkable about this national protest is its scope, its topic, and the way in which postsecondary and secondary students were conflated in both the protest's planning and in reported accounts of the protest. First, the organizers of the protest were explicit that the protest was intended for all students, including primary and secondary students. No attempt was made to distinguish between students based on their age or level of education. Second, never before had a group sought to mobilize across schools on a matter of national importance. Prior to the 1935 peace protest, nearly all student protests were aimed at local decision-makers and sought to influence their decisions. But this protest was aimed at national decision-makers and at shifting public opinions on war in Europe. The prospect of war was deeply personal for these students—many knew that they would be the ones fighting such a war—which grounds the protest in the lived and local concerns of its participants, but the ultimate goal went beyond the local confines of a single school or district. This was a revolutionary idea and began to expand the possibilities for school protests. In many ways, the 1935 peace protest opened the door for the student protests of the 1960s.

The Decade of Protest: Student Protests in the 1960s and Early 1970s

Between 1935 and the 1960s, primary and secondary students continued to protest as they had since at least 1886, but the 1960s—foreshadowed by the nationwide 1935 peace protest—marked a sea change in the scope and prevalence of student protests. In 1968 alone, at the peak of K–12 student protests, there were over 2,000 high school sit-ins, boycotts, and other protests (Swanchak, 1972). The phenomenon was so widespread that, during the 1968–1969 school year, more than half of all junior and senior high schools in the country experienced some form of protest (Dagenais & Marsacuilo, 1972). Importantly, this shift in student protests was not marked by a single campaign or purpose, like the peace protest of 1935. Instead, students were protesting on a variety of social and local issues. Chief among these issues were desegregation and racial or ethnic inequality, the Vietnam War, and a host of local issues that coalesced into a student rights movement. These protests were influenced and informed by the larger social movements of the time and the corresponding massive unrest at college and universities, but these protests were uniquely K–12. They involved high school students and their families protesting at or around their schools, motivated in large part by the schools' policies or the students' day-to-day experiences.

The 1960s were a contentious time both politically and socially, and the student protests of this era reflected—and sometimes even led—these larger struggles. Following the legal campaign to end *de jure* segregation in schools and the NAACP's legal victory at the Supreme Court in *Brown v. Board of Education* in 1954, the desegregation of schools and the educational experiences and opportunities of African American students was a dominant theme of student protests at the time. However, this wasn't the first time that African American students were protesting or that desegregation was the subject of student protests; the first recorded instance of African American students protesting their schools came in 1886 out of New York City. The news article, appearing in *The New York Times*, read in its entirety: "The pupils of the free colored school at Goshen are on strike. They claim that their teacher devoted the whole of one morning to one study, and they refuse to return to school until the matter is satisfactorily arranged" ("Colored Pupils on Strike," 1886, p. 2). As this article indicates, like their White peers, African American students also have a similar tradition of protesting their schools. Similarly, just as African American protests were not a new phenomenon in schools in the 1960s, neither were protests about the racial integration of schools. Prior to the 1960s, there were dozens of protests both promoting and resisting the integration of high schools. In one typical case out of St. Louis, 400 White pupils walked out of their classes on the day that a group of African American students petitioned to enroll in the school ("White Pupils Walk Out in Race Protest," 1949). While protests around desegregation and racial inequality were not a new phenomenon, their scope and prevalence in the 1960s certainly was.

Between 1968 and the fall of 1970, at the peak of K–12 student protests, there were more than 650 racially motivated protests at high schools across the country (Rury & Hill, 2013, p. 502). These protests, aligning closely with the civil rights movement, were predominantly carried out by African American students who sought to either compel integration of segregated schools or promote greater quality and equality of education within their schools. Chicago, for example, experienced both these types of protests during the 1960s (Danns, 2003). In 1963 and again in 1964, a civil rights umbrella organization in Chicago, the Coordinating Council of Community Organizations, organized massive citywide school boycotts in an effort to force desegregation of the city's schools. Nearly 400,000 students, teachers, and concerned citizens participated in these two boycotts. Later, in 1968, after schools began to be desegregated, a group of high school students—supported by their teachers and community leaders—organized another citywide boycott of the schools to protest inequities in the city's schools and the lack of quality education that their schools were providing them. The student organizers for the 1968 protest had participated in the earlier boycotts and had also been active participants with local civil rights groups, even attending an international conference on Black Power in Philadelphia in 1968. Unlike the earlier boycotts that pushed for integration, these students were focused on equality within their schools. They published a manifesto with 12 demands for the Chicago City Schools that focused on diversifying the school and its curriculum as well as increasing its academic rigor (Danns, 2003). The student organizers for this protest were deeply concerned with the quality of their education and with the ways in which African Americans and Black people were represented both in the school and its curriculum. They even asked for additional and more challenging homework.

To realize these demands, the students decided to boycott their schools every Monday until their demands were met. In the first boycott on October 14, 1968, somewhere between 27,000 and 35,000 students participated. On October 21, more than 20,000 students participated, along with approximately 600 teachers (Danns, 2003, p. 145). After this, the Monday protests continued but with fewer participants, due in large part to the protests' successes. On October 17, the superintendent held a press conference agreeing to make the curriculum more inclusive of Black history and to emphasize hiring more African American personnel. In the following year, 17 new African American assistant principals were hired, more vocational courses were offered, new books emphasizing the contributions of Black people were purchased, buildings across the district were renovated, student athletes were offered insurance, and the school board's radio station began broadcasting programming on African American history (Danns, 2002).

Chicago's experience with student protests in 1968 demonstrates many of the themes of African American student protests throughout this time. First, the method and the goals of the Chicago students' protest mirrored those of students across the country. Students throughout the country were walking out or sitting in to protest for better education and for a more culturally responsive curriculum. In another telling example, students at William Penn Senior High School in Pennsylvania, on the day after the assassination of Martin Luther King, Jr., barricaded themselves in the school's auditorium to celebrate King's legacy and to discuss how they could further his cause (Wright, 2003). This sit-in led to the students demanding the incorporation of more Black history into the curriculum, an increase in African American staff, and the equal participation of African American students and families in the school's politics and governance structure.

Second, the Chicago student protests demonstrate the complex interplay between student activists, teachers, and the larger civil rights movement. The Chicago student leaders, before organizing the 1968 protest, had been deeply involved with other local civil rights activities and organizations. They had participated in boycotts of the schools organized by a community organization only a few years earlier. They had learned from these experiences and used that training to formulate their own protest against the elements of Chicago's schools that deeply impacted their lives. They were also supported in their efforts by teachers who joined them on the picket lines. In many ways, the Chicago student protest could be read as a continuation, or a natural outgrowth, of the civil rights movement. But the relationship between student protests and the civil rights movement is much more complicated.

The student protests of the time were not merely building off of the civil rights movement. In important ways, student protests precipitated the larger civil rights movement and informed its course (Hale, 2018a). While traditional narratives of the civil rights movement begin with *Brown v. Board of Education*, Rosa Parks, and the lunch counter sit-ins of 1960 by college students, many of the inciting incidents of the movement involved high school students and K–12 student protests (Hale, 2013). In 1950, African American students in Farmville, Virginia, walked out of their segregated schools. This protest served as an impetus for one of the cases that would later be consolidated and decided by the U.S. Supreme Court in *Brown v. Board of Education*. In Montgomery, Alabama, a student at Booker T. Washington High School, a few weeks before Rosa Parks's planned demonstration, refused to give up her seat on the bus. And in Jackson, Mississippi, before the Freedom Summer Project, more than 500 students staged a walkout of their high schools to demand better facilities (Hale, 2013).

In addition to informing the genesis of the civil rights movements, student protestors also influenced its course, objectives, and pace. As Rury and Hill (2013) argue:

> The surge in African-American student protests during the latter 1960s and early 1970s can be interpreted as an adjunct to the larger Civil Rights Movement, an echo that refracted through the experiences of students as they encountered racial hostility from whites and deplorable conditions in the schools, particularly

in larger cities but elsewhere too. It can also be seen as a time of greater awareness among high school students regarding racial injustice, especially as it
affected their own lives, and a willingness to confront injustice directly and
forcefully. Thus, while many were drawn into social protest by mainstream
organisations such as the NAACP, they emerged as independent actors, often
critical of old guard civil rights activism and the dominance of middle-class
ideologies. (p. 506)

As "independent actors," the students of this time were informed by the
civil rights movement, but they often acted outside or parallel to that movement as they protested against their schools to challenge the racial inequalities they experienced there. This was particularly true in desegregation
efforts, where student protests provided both the impetus and the resolve for
school desegregation, outside of legal challenges and court-ordered desegregation (Bundy, 2017).

Another instance in which high school student protests provided the
catalyst and focus for a larger social movement can be seen in the Chicano
civil rights movement of the 1960s and '70s. In 1968 in East Los Angeles,
California, over 10,000 Chicano students staged a collective "blowout" of
their high schools (Muñoz, 2018). These students walked out of their schools,
protesting what the students saw as the schools' inferior quality and the district's racist practices and curriculum. Motivating this protest were the district's policies and practices that had resulted in Mexican American students
having lower achievement, repeating more grades, having a lower graduation
rate, and being segregated from their white peers (Gutierrez, 1996). Similar
to African American student protests at the time, the Los Angeles students
demanded improved educational opportunities, a curriculum that was more
representative of Chicano culture and history, and greater representation in
school staff and faculty. This massive student protest launched the Chicano
civil rights movement and spawned similar protests throughout the country
(Barrera, 2004; Muñoz, 2018).

Protests for racial and ethnic justice were not the only student protests
during the 1960s. Students at the time, in many ways echoing their college
peers, also staged mass demonstrations against the Vietnam War and on a
host of other social and political issues that impacted their lives (Graham,
2006). On April 26, 1968, reminiscent of the national 1935 peace protest,
an estimated 1 million students from colleges and high schools across the
country walked out of their schools to protest the Vietnam War (Graham,
2006). Even while students were protesting the national draft and the United
States' involvement in Vietnam, they were also protesting against a variety of local policies and practices that influenced their experiences within
schools, coalescing into a national student rights movement.

Similar to their predecessors, students in the 1960s protested against
policies and practices that deeply impacted them. However, unlike their

predecessors' actions, these protests directly challenged and addressed the social and legal status of students as children and young adults in schools. Students in the 1960s launched protests against restrictive school dress codes that forced boys to wear their hair short or girls to wear skirts or dresses, asserting that such rules violated their freedom of self-expression. They challenged censorship of student speech and student publications, arguing that such rules violated their free speech rights. They protested their lack of voice in determining school policies and practices, arguing that this violated their equal rights as citizens (Graham, 2006). These protests were directed locally, but they informed a national movement of students making the same claims against their own schools. This was perhaps not a movement in the same way that the civil rights movement was, but the breadth of student protests certainly made it a national phenomenon with national results. The student rights movement led to significant Supreme Court decisions and other policy changes that recognized and defined student rights in schools as formalized in *Tinker v. Des Moines* (1969), which recognized student free speech rights; *Goss v. Lopez* (1975), which extended due process protections to students; and *New Jersey v. T.L.O.* (1983), which acknowledged that students have protected privacy rights in schools.

Additionally, like the student protests during the late 1800s following the common school movement, the student activism of the 1960s also aligned with broad societal beliefs about the purposes of education in cultivating democratic citizenship. Similar arguments to those made by Thomas Jefferson and Horace Mann about the civic goals of education were picked up by the courts during this time as they ended legal segregation, established students' rights, and expanded educational access for all. In perhaps the most significant U.S. Supreme Court case of the 20th century, *Brown v. Board of Education* (1954), the Supreme Court struck down the racial segregation of schools in part due to the important role of education in a democratic society. The Court, recognizing the important role of education in cultivating democratic citizenship, wrote:

> [E]ducation is perhaps the most important function of state and local governments. Compulsory school attendance laws and the great expenditures for education both demonstrate our recognition of the importance of education to our democratic society. It is the very foundation of good citizenship. (p. 493)

Similarly, in *Tinker v. Des Moines* (1969), the case that established students' speech rights in schools, the Supreme Court reiterated "that [public schools] are educating the young for citizenship is reason for scrupulous protection of Constitutional freedoms of the individual, if we are not to strangle the free mind at its source and teach youth to discount important principles of our government as mere platitudes" (p. 507, quoting *West Virginia v. Barnette*, 1943). The Court's decisions in *Brown* and *Tinker* echo the long tradition in American history of viewing schools as serving the civic purpose of preparing students for democratic citizenship. The student protesters at this time, especially those like the students who brought the *Tinker* case who were suspended for protesting the Vietnam War, were both advancing and living the civic purpose of education.

While still advancing the civic goals of education in the United States, the student protests of the 1960s were quantitatively and qualitatively different from those prior to 1960 in their scope, goals, and achievements. However, it is less clear what accounted for these changes and for the subsequent drop-off of student protests in the 1970s. Social causes for the "age of protest" during the 1960s and the parallel protests of high school students are complex. Sherkat and Blocker (1994) and Harrison (1993) outline numerous causes for why these protests occurred, including (1) the confluence of significant historical events, like *Brown* and the Vietnam War; (2) the socialization of students and community leaders as they interacted with other successful protests both nationally and globally; and (3) the characteristics of the rising generation of the 1960s, namely their belief in their ability to shape the world, an orientation toward community, and the confidence that came from growing up in one of the most economically prosperous periods in American history. Other scholars have pointed to a rise in "activist subcultures" that informed a general feeling of antiauthoritarianism (Van Dyke, 1998), greater access by minorities and other oppressed groups to political and social institutions (Muñoz, 2018), and a growing political awareness of the disconnect between nationally significant principles and practice (Rury & Hill, 2013) to explain the rise in protests of this time.

Perhaps the most compelling explanation for the rise and prevalence of student protests during the 1960s lies in the changing social expectations for adolescents and their institutional position within schools. Following World War II, high school became a near universal expectation for young people, leading to a prolonging of adolescence. In effect, the students of the 1960s were the first generation of students compelled to forgo adulthood while attending institutions that granted them little freedom (Swanchak, 1972). They were encouraged to spend a longer time in identity formation but were denied avenues to participate in society due to their marginal role as students and children. Under this theory, students protested because they were politically impotent, even as they were encouraged to develop civic identities and were deeply concerned with the social problems that impacted their lives (Ohlsen, 1971). Read against this tradition, these student protests can be seen as an "unprecedented and self-conscious effort [by students] to redefine their status and roles . . . to shed some of the limitations of childhood and gain greater control over their lives" (Graham, 2006, p. 9). While students at the time weren't necessarily attempting to "shed the limitations of childhood," but were rather resisting the imposition of those limits, this account does offer an important insight into why the student protests of the 1960s, especially the student rights movement, happened as they did. Although there was likely no single cause of the social upheaval and sustained student protests of the 1960s, each of the social phenomena discussed likely contributed to this age of protest and helps explain why the protests trickled off in the 1970s.

The most obvious reason that student protests dwindled in the 1970s was because the protests of the 1960s were widely successful in shifting policy and public opinion. Protests, alongside sustained legal challenges, led to school integration and the end of *de jure* segregation. The student protesters of the civil rights movement and the Chicano civil rights movement were successful in compelling school officials to make schools more equitable and to improve the educational opportunities of minority students (Rury & Hill, 2013). The student rights movement was successful in shaping high schools to be more tolerant of student voice and expression and shifted schools to be more responsive to students (Graham, 2006). In addition, sustained public pressure led to the withdrawal of U.S. troops from Vietnam, ending U.S. military involvement in the war. In many ways, the protests of the 1960s stopped because they worked.

However, there were other reasons the protests of the 1960s faded. Public responses to the protests were often hostile. Many people at the time saw student protests as illegitimate challenges to adult authority and thought that students were pushing for special rights that were undeserved and incompatible with childhood (Ransford, 1972). These responses echo earlier responses to student protests that saw these activities as incompatible with the efficient operation of schools as well as the inculcation of industrial values that many saw as a primary goal of public education. These attitudes, as well as strong resistance from conservative groups who were opposed to these often radically liberal protests, led to an increase in the punitive structure of schools and to the criminalization of protest writ large in many places (Gillen, 2009). This fear of increased sanctions, coupled with a decreased urgency due to many of the different movements' successes, likely led to a decrease in student protests. Also significant was the economic downturn of the early 1970s and '80s. As students and their families became less financially secure—and schools came to be seen as more necessary mechanisms for obtaining economic advancement—students became more concerned with their economic survival and could no longer afford the increased consequences that now accompanied student disobedience (Johnston, 2015). But, while the scope and prevalence of student protests in the 1960s did not continue into the 1970s and beyond, these protests continued a tradition of student activism from at least the 1880s and that continued—and continues—to motivate students to speak out against their schools and society at large.

BUSINESS AS USUAL OR THE CALM BEFORE THE STORM? STUDENT PROTESTS FROM 1974 TO THE PARKLAND PROTESTS

Primary and secondary student protests may have reached their zenith in 1968, but they have never fully disappeared. Similar to the period between 1886 and 1935, students during the late 1970s to mid-2010s continued to protest against their local schools in response to local decisions and policies that had important ramifications for their experiences within school. Like their predecessors before 1935, these students were protesting against things like the dismissal of a favorite teacher or inadequate learning conditions (Garza, 1990). But, like the students in the 1960s, they were also often protesting systemic issues that found expression in their schools. This often included issues surrounding discriminatory employment decisions, racial inequalities in schools, or ideological struggles over what should be including in the school curriculum.

As the history of K–12 student protests demonstrates, the student protests following the Parkland shooting in 2018 are part of a long tradition of student activism. Like the student protestors who came before them, the students who engaged in these protests banded together to protest policies and practices that deeply affected their lives in schools. These students had grown up in school climates during the early 2000s in which the threat of gun violence was a common concern. They had experienced the effects of numerous national school shootings, endured active-shooter drills, experienced heightened school safety and harsher disciplinary regimes, and become accustomed to seeing armed school resource officers in their schools. The students who engaged in the protests following the Parkland shooting were speaking back to these policies and the ways in which these policies had impacted their experiences at school. They added a voice that had been missing from the political debate, one that had been silenced but was deeply affected by its outcomes.

Additionally, like the protests of the 1960s, these protests occurred against the backdrop of other national movements and protests and were informed by these groups, even as they applied those lessons through the lens of their unique experiences. In this way, these students were not only engaged with local concerns but were also part of a larger societal movement to end gun violence in the United States. The deep connection between the student protests and other advocacy groups can be seen in the first student protests of the spring of 2018, the #ENOUGH national school walkouts. These demonstrations were organized by the Women's March, an organization aimed toward promoting women's perspectives and addressing issues that impact women in American politics. The other student protests of the spring of 2018, one organized by the students of Parkland and the other begun as a Change.org petition, were independent of the Women's March's protests but were certainly influenced by it, demonstrating again how students often extend and impact larger social movements. Indeed, more than a year after the Parkland shooting and the national protests that they organized, March For Our Lives (n.d.-b)—the organization begun by Parkland students to end gun violence in America—announced a "Peace Plan for a Safer America" in preparation of the 2020 presidential election. The students of the 2018 student protests continue to impact and engage with politics and larger social movements in America.

Finally, the student protests of 2018 also continued a long relationship between student and teacher activism. Throughout the history of student protests, students have influenced, empowered, and supported their teachers even as their teachers did the same for them. While the student protests and teacher strikes of the spring of 2018 dealt with different issues and pursued different goals, each group supported the other as they sought larger societal change. To understand this relationship more deeply, the next chapter turns to the history of teacher civic activism in the United States.

CHAPTER 3

Teacher Civic Activism in American History

Like students, teachers also have a long history of civic activism in the United States. This history is deeply connected with the history of teachers' labor unions and often involves struggles between teacher unions and local boards of education. In many cases, teacher civic activism arose as teachers and their unions sought greater teacher professionalism through demands for collective bargaining rights, job protections, higher salaries, and the ability to self-regulate the teaching profession. Often opposed to these requests were local school officials who wanted to retain local control of education and leave school policy decisions with locally elected officials (Scribner, 2015). These conflicts directly pitted teachers against schools and raised complicated issues of the role of teachers in politics as well as questions of who should make educational decisions. In addition to the rise of labor unions, 19th-century societal beliefs that characterized teaching as women's work are also deeply intertwined with the history of teachers' civic activism. After the feminization of the teaching force in the late 1800s, teachers were subject to depressed wages and constrained professionalism, including widespread laws that required female teachers to resign upon getting married. This both motivated and limited teachers as they sought to garner recognition of teaching as a profession, with the societal esteem and autonomy that accompanied it. Finally, the history of teacher unions is also deeply connected with issues of educational equality and quality. Prior to the civil rights movement, teachers and their associations, especially Black teachers' association in the South, were often among the first groups agitating for educational and societal equality. Teachers' unions in the late 20th century, however, often had complicated relationships with school reforms aimed at racial equality. The arc of teachers' civic activism is informed by these three larger societal movements—the professionalization of teaching, the feminization of teaching, and the struggle for equality—but peppered throughout this history are deep and enduring connections to student civic activism.

A PERIOD OF INCUBATION: TEACHER CIVIC ACTIVISM UNTIL THE 1940s

While students have been protesting for as long as there have been schools, the same cannot be said for teachers. What may have been the first teacher strike in the United States occurred in 1902, well into the proliferation of common schools in the United States. Reported in *The New York Times*, this strike involved 15 teachers who refused to return to work until the school board paid them the salaries they were owed (See Figure 3.1). These teachers formed a "compact union," and—if the article is to be believed— with the help of their "brothers and men friends," were able to prevent out- side teachers from replacing them. Ultimately, these teachers were successful in leveraging an existing law to obtain part of their back salaries, though the article foreshadows an important limitation to teachers' collective action: "the influence of the children's parents" and perceived tensions between teachers' self-interest and the public good.

Although the first widely reported strike may have occurred in 1902, teacher strikes did not become common until the 1960s. Prior to this, at least three interconnected societal forces worked to suppress teacher civic activism. First, before the mid–20th century, teaching was seen as a tem- porary occupation rather than a professional career. This stemmed in part from America's early schools, which were largely seasonal and therefore

Figure 3.1. "Teachers' Strike Off."

TEACHERS' STRIKE OFF.

Law Comes to Aid Fifteen Young Women Who Went Out at Pittston.
Special to The New York Time.

WILKESBARRE, March 25.—The fifteen school teachers, all young women, who have been on strike in Pittston Township for the last four months, went back to the school today, and brought to an end the long vacation of their 1.400 pupils. The strike began last November. It was due to the fact that the Directors could not pay salaries, having spent the money for other things. To the fifteen was due over $6,000. They organized a compact union and went out. Other teachers could not be procured because the strikers had brothers and men friends, and there was no money in the school treasury. One got married, and another is preparing to go into a convent.

The strike ended because the township would have been entirely without school money from the State should it not, according to law, keep the schools open for seven months of the year. In order to save this appropriation, the Direc- tors finally agreed to assign the full amount of it to the teachers. It is only $3,100 and not enough to pay half their back salaries, but the influence of the children's parents was brought to bear, and they agreed to return to their desks. The Direc- tors have also promised to pay all they owe as soon as possible.

Note. First published in *The New York Times* on March 26, 1902.

offered only limited employment opportunities. These early teaching positions were often thought to be well suited to young, educated men in order for them to earn a little money before starting their proper careers. Because of these factors, during the 19th century, the average teaching career was between 2 to 3 years (Strober & Tyack, 1980). Even after schooling began to be a year-long endeavor following the establishment of public common schools, ideas about teaching as a temporary occupation continued, fueled by the feminization of the teaching profession.

During the mid-1800s, women were hired to be teachers at higher rates than men such that women came to dominate the teaching profession in the early 1900s. This shift was caused by a confluence of factors. There were teacher shortages due to greater demands for teachers, stemming from the vast expansion of public schooling during this time. Young men of the time had more employment opportunities, further exacerbating teacher shortages. Greater numbers of schools and broader access to education led to increased educational opportunities for women, which in turn led to more women being more highly educated, though they had only limited employment opportunities available to them. Finally, there was a national ideological shift that came to understand the nature of teaching as being within the "women's sphere" and as good preparation for motherhood. Taken together, these factors led to the feminization of the teaching profession, though they did not disrupt the dominance of men in school administration (Strober & Tyack, 1980).

As a result of this feminization of teaching, teachers in the early parts of the 20th century were often underpaid, which furthered the feminization of teaching as more and more women teachers were hired in an attempt to lower educational costs. Additionally, this shift led to teachers being excluded from civic participation and subjected to stringent external regulations—even as teaching gave women an important avenue to begin acting within political spaces on behalf of schools, children, and mothers (Cowles, 2014). One example of how these ideas, coupled with the conception of teaching as a temporary occupation, found expression in policy were in state and district requirements that women teachers retire after getting married. These policies were commonplace until the late 1960s; in 1930, 60% of urban districts had bans on hiring married women teachers (Donahue, 2002). Not only were these policies based on ideas about teaching as women's work and the proper role of women in society, but they also perpetuated ideas about teaching as being a temporary occupation without the respect and protections afforded a professional career.

The final limitation to teachers engaging in civic activism during this time were widely held beliefs about the civic responsibilities of public employees and the idea that teachers were engaged in public service. Because teachers were engaged in public service, any attempt to prioritize the power or individual well-being of teachers was seen as inimical to teachers' duties to promote the public good, an idea that persists and has been repurposed by the A Nation at Risk paradigm. These ideas found expression in teachers' lack of collective bargaining rights and their inability to legally strike. From this perspective, teachers were civil servants whose sole responsibility was to the public. Engaging in labor disputes, or even engaging with organized labor at all, was seen as a violation of the teacher's public duty. This sentiment was captured in one contemporary commentator's criticism of threatened teacher unionization and a potential strike in Chicago:

> In the event of another strike in the erection of school buildings, what would be the attitude of the members of the Chicago Teachers' federation if they retain their affiliation with these labor organizations? That their sympathies would be with the strikers and their moral and political influence would be thrown into the scale against the very board of education they serve is manifest from the reciprocal obligations they have assumed by this affiliation. ("Fear of Teacher Strike Prompted Loeb Rule," 1916, p. 18)

Here, the commentator viewed belonging to a union and promoting the rights and interests of workers as being fundamentally incompatible with the teachers' duty to the board of education. Teachers, by the nature of their chosen positions, owed obligations to the school board and the public interest it served. Agitating against the interests of the school board or engaging with a union to improve the political position or well-being of teachers was seen as violating those obligations.

These attitudes—coupled with the laws they informed that forbade public employees' collective bargaining rights and criminalized public employee strikes throughout the United States—greatly limited the willingness and ability of teachers' unions to organize and advocate. Because of this reticence, while the two largest national teachers' associations were formed during this time, they were not widespread and often actively resisted engaging in local strikes.

The National Education Association (NEA) was founded in 1870 when the National Teachers Association merged with the American Normal School Association, the National Association of School Superintendents, and the Central College Association (Strom, 1979). Until the 1960s, the NEA avoided labor-style strikes. This reluctance was due in part to both the perception that teacher involvement in politics was a threat to the professionalization of teachers (Toloudis, 2019) and the ways in which, until the 1970s, the NEA was structured to privilege the perspectives and interests of school administrators over those of teachers (Urban, 1993). Instead of promoting teacher strikes to realize professional protections for teachers such as tenure, the NEA engaged in advocacy and lobbying, coupled with threatened boycotts and sanctions where they would instruct their members to resign or not accept work in certain districts or states (Scribner, 2015).

Until the 1960s, these methods were often successful, though their impact was geographically limited. For example, in 1909, New Jersey passed the nation's first teacher tenure law, which granted due process protections to teachers prior to termination, after the state's NEA-affiliated teacher association threatened mass teacher resignations (Donahue, 2002). However, by 1920, only five states had teacher tenure laws, and only 22% of teachers were covered by state tenure laws in 1930 (Donahue, 2002).

Finding its genesis in teachers' concerns over a lack of militancy in the NEA, the American Federation of Teachers (AFT) was founded in 1916 with strong connections to organized labor (Strom, 1979). From its inception, the AFT was more willing to engage in direct action to achieve its goals. The first AFT local chapter was the Chicago Teachers' Federation (CTF), which was founded in 1897 to oppose political threats to recently enacted teachers' pension laws (Rousmaniere, 2005). Prior to becoming a part of the AFT in 1916, the CTF engaged in protracted direct action to realize greater funding for education. While the AFT found its origins in organizations like the CFT and continued their commitment to direct action, AFT-led teacher strikes were sporadic in the early 1900s and often ran afoul of dominant beliefs about teachers and their obligations to the public, frequently to the detriment of the protesting teachers. As an example, in 1920, 100 teachers in Lancaster, Pennsylvania, formed an AFT affiliate in order to seek salary increases from the local board of education. The board refused their request and did not reappoint any of the teachers at the end of the year despite a practice of renewing all teachers' contracts. The teachers appealed this decision to the state superintendent. Expressing the belief that union membership was inimical to teacher's public duty, the superintendent held that, not only were the board's actions lawful, but the teachers were unfit to teach due to their affiliation with the AFT (Toloudis, 2019). The superintendent's decision demonstrates how public perception often viewed teachers' organizations and labor actions as pitting teachers' special interests against the public interest. Within this formulation, teachers' special interests were required to yield to the public interest.

These limitations meant that there were only isolated incidents of teacher strikes during this time, mostly focused on enforcing teacher contracts and protesting employment decisions. In an early example from 1910, demonstrating both a common impetus for these early activities and their limited methods, 25 of a school's 40 teachers resigned in protest of the school board's decision to not rehire the superintendent ("School Teachers Strike," 1910). Even during this period of limited teacher's strikes, though, there were often connections between teacher and student civic activism. In one instance out of Muncie, Indiana, in 1920, students engaged in a 1-day walkout of their high school in solidarity with their teachers' demand for higher pay ("Muncie Students Strike to Raise Pay for Teachers," 1920). While it was often the case that students' activities were aligned with those of their teachers, this was not always the case. In 1936, 2,500 students in Jasper, Alabama, went on strike to pressure teachers into joining an affiliate of the AFT ("Teachers Defiant in Student Strike," 1936). The protest arose after three teachers in the county were discharged for union activity. Due to the lack of protections for organized labor, this was a legal employment practice at the time. The students, rather than the teachers, protested these firings in hope of putting pressure on the local teachers to unionize, even though 98% of the teachers had adopted a resolution that challenged efforts to force them to become members of the AFT.

Ultimately, teacher strikes were in their infancy in the period leading up to 1940. The few teacher strikes that did occur were local in scope and were often directed toward ensuring that teachers received the basic benefits of their employment. However, even during this time, teachers began to exercise their collective power in pursuit of job protections and other trappings of professionalism. Following the passage of the Wagner Act in 1935, which gave collective bargaining rights and fair labor practices to private employees, and the adoption of more aggressive tactics by the AFT, the period between the 1940s and the 1960s saw a steady rise in teacher strikes.

THE RISE OF TEACHERS' UNIONS: THE GROWING TEACHER STRIKES OF 1940 THROUGH THE EARLY 1960s

In the period between 1940 and 1966, there were at least 129 teacher strikes that led to work stoppages (Glass, 1967). Teachers during this time were predominately protesting for greater salaries, more job protections, and workers' rights, such as union recognition and the right to bargain collectively. However, these teachers continued to run up against ideological as well as legal barriers to their activities. Prior to the 1960s, most states did not require that local school boards recognize and engage in collective bargaining with teachers' organizations. In some states, like Massachusetts, Michigan, and Rhode Island, school boards were mandated to collectively bargain with teachers' unions. In at least one state, California, school boards were forbidden from doing so. For other states, though, the decision of whether to recognize and negotiate with teachers' unions was left to the local school district, often with mixed results (Seitz, 1966). Additionally, strikes by governmental employees were prohibited at the federal level and in many states until the 1970s, with at least 16 states still forbidding the practice in 1967. These prohibitions, even though they were often toothless and difficult to enforce, depressed teacher civic activism (Neirynck, 1967). Together, these legal limitations, coupled with persistent ideological beliefs surrounding teaching as a feminine, temporary occupation with a duty toward the public good, continued to limit teacher civic activism at this time, even as teacher strikes became more frequent.

The rise of teacher strikes during this time was attributable to a number of interrelated causes. First, the AFT's successful use of teacher strikes to achieve favorable outcomes for its members began putting pressure on the NEA to adopt more militant strategies. The need to effectively compete for new members, coupled with a decrease in the effectiveness of the NEA's boycott strategy, led the NEA to adopt strikes as a legitimate form of advocacy (Neirynck, 1967). This in turn validated teacher strikes and led to their rise nationwide. For example, in 1961, New York City's teachers elected the United Federation of Teachers, an affiliate of the AFT, as their sole bargaining representative. The following year, the UFT staged a 1-day strike of New York's schools with over 20,000 teachers participating. After the strike, the UFT was able to achieve a favorable collective bargaining agreement for its members (Glass, 1967). This success gave the AFT, a much smaller national organization with approximately 125,000 members compared to the NEA's nearly 1,000,000 members in 1967 (Glass, 1967), national recognition and put pressure on the NEA to achieve similar results for its members. Further exacerbating this shift, at around the same time, the NEA had suffered a widely publicized failure in its advocacy efforts in Florida when its threatened statewide boycott and sanctions failed to motivate state legislators to raise education spending and teacher salaries (Scribner, 2015). Together, these factors led the NEA to shift its focus from state-level to district-level advocacy and to embrace teachers' strikes in order to compete for members with the AFT. It was also during this time that the NEA came to be more responsive to teachers' interests as teachers supplanted school administrators in determining the policies and direction of the NEA (Urban, 1993). The competition between the AFT and the newly teacher-centric NEA led to a greater number of strikes nationwide. In many ways, this shift led teachers away from agitating for the public, as the NEA had done with its boycotts and policy work, and toward a labor militancy that was directed more at advancing teachers' private interests (Glass, 1967).

The rise in teacher strikes from 1940 to the 1960s also corresponded with greater legal recognition of unions for public employees and greater employment protections for teachers. The success of teacher strikes in achieving these goals facilitated further strikes. Of the 129 teacher strikes between 1940 and 1966, 29 were directed toward union organization, with goals such as gaining recognition of a union, requiring collective bargaining, or preventing discrimination and retaliation against union members. Forty-five of the strikes during this time were directed more broadly at issues surrounding job security and working conditions for teachers (Glass, 1967). In part because of these teachers' activities, by 1970 most states had authorized school districts to collectively bargain with teachers' unions (Strom, 1979), and many states had passed laws granting teachers stronger job protections like tenure and prohibitions against discrimination based on marital status (Donahue, 2002). The U.S. Supreme Court also contributed to the decriminalization of teacher strikes with its decision in *Pickering v. Board of Education* (1968). In this case, the Court reinstated a teacher who had been terminated after writing a letter to the editor criticizing the school board, holding that the letter was protected speech under the First Amendment. This loosening of legal restrictions for teachers aligned with a larger societal recognition of the validity and legality of public sector unions. In 1962, President Kennedy signed Executive Order 10988, which granted employees in federal service the right to organize and collectively bargain (Glass, 1967). In light of this national shift, many states at this time also loosened legal restrictions on public sector unions, which in part led to a tripling of public employee strikes from 1965 to 1966 (Glass, 1967).

TEACHERS AND THE DECADE OF PROTEST: THE MID-1960s TO EARLY 1970s

The upsurge in teacher strikes in the 1960s corresponded with larger societal movements that also relied on civic activism, such as the civil rights movement, the protests against the Vietnam War, and the student rights movement. In many ways, the years between the mid-1960s and early '70s were the decade of protests. There were thousands of protests throughout the United States at this time, and teachers were just another element of society that engaged in these activities. However, teachers were not merely just riding the wave of societal unrest. Teachers' activism also contributed to and propelled these larger societal movements. Not only did teachers protest alongside their students in opposition to the Vietnam War and in support of the students rights movement, but teachers often empowered their students to agitate for societal change through their pedagogical and curricular choices.

Teachers during this time, especially African American teachers in the South, promoted larger societal movements through their professional organizations and their teaching (Loder-Jackson, 2015). In the South, prior to the civil rights movement, African American teachers—acting through their professional organizations—engaged in concerted social activism to promote equitable education. In one prominent early example, the Black Georgia Teachers and Education Association, not without personal risk to its members, engaged in a prolonged fact-finding and petition campaign to encourage state lawmakers to pass a 1919 bill aimed at providing increased school opportunities for all Georgia students (Walker, 2005).

In addition to lobbying policymakers, African American teacher activists engaged in activities that precipitated and informed legal challenges to school inequalities, like the *Brown v. Board of Education* case, and—through their teaching—they empowered their students to engage in the emerging civil rights movement (Walker, 2013). As Hale (2018b) writes:

> The history of Black teacher associations illustrates a pedagogical and intellectual activism that was subtle, yet equally present in imbuing young people with a critical consciousness to challenge Jim Crow. Black educators developed social and political networks built on donated time, labor and private resources committed to the development of public schools and placed the demand for a quality education on the larger agenda of the Civil Rights Movement. Teachers practiced other tenets of intellectual and pedagogical activism that included implementing a curriculum, extracurricular courses, and a culturally relevant education in Black schools during the era of segregation. Teaching behind closed doors and developing their profession inculcated a sense of resistance throughout segregated Black schools across the South that resonated deeply with the principles of the Civil Rights Movement. While not on the front lines of the movement, teachers transformed their profession into a viable and political site of resistance. (p. 454)

Through their activities, teachers at this time both informed the larger civil rights movement and prepared and empowered their students to take part in it (Baker, 2011; Frederick & View, 2009).

However, not all teacher activism during this time promoted the emerging civil rights movement. In many ways, as teacher unions sought to advance the private interests of their members rather than broader conceptions of the public good, this set the stage for teacher activism to be indirectly, and sometimes directly, opposed to the goals of larger social movements like the civil rights movement. In 1968, New York City teachers again engaged in a teacher strike, this time in response to the actions of the Ocean Hill-Brownsville governing board in transferring, hiring, and firing district teachers (Strom, 1979; Urofsky, 1970). New York's teacher union, the United Federation of Teachers (UFT), saw these actions as a threat to the job security of its members, which led to prolonged teachers' strikes that directly pitted teacher professionalism against the local control of the schools by the school board. While the teachers eventually secured greater teacher protections, this success resulted in an eroding of local control, particularly for minority groups who were concentrated in the area (Strom, 1979). As teachers throughout the United States joined larger labor organizations in higher numbers and adopted labor's ideologies and rhetoric, this "culminated in the transformation of big-city educators into highly organized and militant labor unionists, whose industrial-based approaches to securing worker protections through collective bargaining impeded the progress of important urban educational reforms" (Alvarez, 2003). Ultimately, the conflict between teachers' unions pursuing their own self-interest and different conceptions of the public good would set the stage for the era of teacher strikes following the 1960s and '70s.

MODERN TEACHER STRIKES: TEACHER UNIONS AND THE EMERGENCE OF NEOLIBERALISM, 1974–PRESENT

By the late 1970s, 72% of all public school teachers were members of organizations that engaged in collective bargaining with their employers (Thornton, 1982). Between the 1970s and the late 2000s, that number remained largely consistent, with 76% of all public school teachers belonging to a labor union or association in 2007–2008 (National Center for Education Statistics [NCES], n.d.). This increase in teachers' participation in labor unions and more permissive legal and social attitudes toward teacher strikes led to teacher strikes being a common and persistent occurrence following the 1960s (Scribner, 2015). Indeed, between the mid-1970s through the 1980s, there were approximately 100 teacher strikes a year in the United States (Murphy, 1992). However, while teacher unions achieved significant gains in consolidating and codifying their political authority prior to the 1980s, the rise of conservative politics and a national recession in the United States in the 1980s led to a narrowing of these political gains (Schirmer, 2017). Teachers' unions in the 1960s and '70s succeeded in achieving legal recognition for unions, collective bargaining rights, and due process protections for teachers, but—through focusing their collective efforts on changing legal authorities—teacher unions were susceptible to changes in those policies and often neglected to cultivate broad coalitions and grassroots efforts that would be necessary to prevent subsequent limitations in their legal rights (Shelton, 2017).

Since teachers achieved legal recognitions and protections, many states have passed "right to work" laws that limit the legal authority of unions to collectively bargain. In addition, the U.S. Supreme Court, through a series of judicial decisions relying on the First Amendment rights of workers, has eroded the authority of unions by limiting their ability to spend union dues on political activities and collect agency fees from nonunion members represented by mandatory collective bargaining agreements (*Knox v. Service Employees International Union*, 2012; *Janus v. AFSCME*, 2018). Taken together, as discussed more fully in the next chapter, these shifts in policy and a general societal cynicism toward government and public employees spurred by conservative politics (including the A Nation at Risk paradigm in education) since the 1980s have placed teachers and their unions in a position where their civic activism is seen as inimical to larger policy reform movements aimed at improving education, like school choice and accountability mechanisms such as merit pay. It is within this context that the statewide teacher strikes of the spring of 2018 occurred as teachers, both led by and leading their unions, reacted to the effects of these shifts and the ways in which teachers have been positioned within contemporary educational policy.

PUTTING THE 2018 STUDENT PROTESTS AND TEACHER STRIKES
INTO HISTORICAL CONTEXT

The student protests and teacher strikes of 2018 were a continuation of their respective histories of civic activism, but, at the same time, they also interrupted recent trends and dominant political ideologies. Like the teacher strikes leading up to the 1960s, the 2018 teacher strikes often involved teachers' collective action for the public good, even as they were pursuing private goals as well. The teachers engaged in these strikes were advocating not only for increases in teacher compensation but also for greater funding for education in general. This, as well as their often tangential relationship to established teacher unions, positioned these teachers in ways that were supportive of local schools rather than as antagonistic toward them. Further, by focusing on grassroots movements and collective action directed at state governments, these teacher strikes harkened back to earlier teacher movements directed at organizing teachers' collective political power and interrupted the legal rights focus that teachers' unions had adopted after the 1970s.

The student protesters of 2018 were engaged in a political movement reminiscent of the social movements of the 1960s. Like their predecessors, these students were protesting larger societal issues that had immediate and profound impacts on their lives. Also like their predecessors, these students were engaging in civic activism in a climate of larger societal protests, like those being conducted by their teachers.

As the history of teacher and student civic activism demonstrates, students and teachers have a shared and interconnected tradition of civic activism in the United States. Throughout this history, students and teachers have often protested with and on behalf of each other and supported each other, even while they each pursued their own goals. From students protesting the unfair removal of teachers in the 1930s and motivating teachers to form professional organizations to help protect their interests, to teachers advocating on behalf of their students and teaching them in ways that empowered their civic activism prior to the civil rights movement, there are deep connections between student and teacher activism throughout American history. In addition to these deep connections, the parallel traditions of student and teacher protest also share a history of reacting to and informing larger societal movements, like the 2018 protests did with the A Nation at Risk paradigm that has come to dominate American educational policy. The teacher strikes and student protests of 2018 were both implicit and explicit rejections of the political context that has arisen from the A Nation at Risk paradigm. The next chapter explores this dominant policy paradigm and explores the ways in which it has impacted—though not eliminated—student and teacher civic agency.

CHAPTER 4

The A Nation at Risk Paradigm and Student and Teacher Civic Agency

The student protests and teacher strikes of the spring of 2018 were remarkable. Not only were they the most prominent recent entries in a long history of student and teacher activism but they also occurred within a political climate in education that is antagonistic toward student and teacher civic agency. Since at least the 1980s, educational policy in the United States has been dominated by a loose coalition of conservative ideologies (Apple, 2006). These ideologies have given rise to the A Nation at Risk paradigm, named after the 1983 federal report that argued that the lamentable state of America's schools threatened its economic and political dominance (Mehta, 2013). This paradigm—and the coalition of conservative ideologies that inform it—understand education as serving the production of human capital; students are educated to increase their capacity for work in order to increase the economic well-being of the economy (Spring, 2011).

Ironically, while the educational paradigm that has developed since 1983 can be traced to the *A Nation at Risk* report and its rhetoric connecting economic competition and educational success, the report itself did not mandate this outcome. Indeed, *A Nation at Risk* was issued as a subtle rejection of some of the policy prescriptions that would come to dominate the paradigm. It also proposed reforms that contradict the paradigm's later outcomes. The report was the result of the National Commission on Excellence in Education, which was created by the U.S. Secretary of Education, Terrel Bell, during the presidency of Ronald Reagan. President Reagan's educational policy agenda was focused on promoting school prayer, creating tuition tax credits or vouchers to facilitate school choice, and eradicating the federal Department of Education to reduce the influence of federal intervention in educational policy (Mehta, 2015). Against this political backdrop, the *A Nation at Risk* report's rhetoric and recommendations can be read as a subtle pushback against President Reagan's educational policy. The report recommended a focus on educating for the "the New Basics"—subjects like math, science, English, and social studies—to ensure educational excellence for all students. To accomplish this goal, the report called for extended school days and a longer school year, increased testing, and greater teacher professionalism, including higher licensure standards and increased pay. Instead of leading to the elimination of the Department of Education, these recommendations actually facilitated greater federal involvement in education. In addition, the report's recommendations for professionalizing teachers are at odds with the paradigm's effect of eroding teacher control and autonomy.

Ultimately, however, it was the rhetoric of *A Nation at Risk* that has most influenced educational policy since 1983. The report warned of a "rising tide of mediocrity" in America's schools that threatened America's future. To support this connection, the report reasoned that "[education] undergirds American prosperity, security, and civility" and that "[America's] once unchallenged preeminence in commerce, industry, science, and technological innovation is being overtaken by competitors throughout the world." Under this logic, America's declining educational quality was responsible for its declining international position. Thus, "the report linked the future of the nation's international economic competitiveness with the reform of its educational system" (Mehta, 2015, p. 21). Within this formulation, as America's economic and cultural strength relative to the rest of the world was thought to diminish during the 1980s, the report cited America's schools as the cause. This framing of the state of education in the United States and the connections between education and the economy would become defining features of the A Nation at Risk paradigm.

The A Nation at Risk paradigm, with its emphasis on economic development, often conflicts with another commonly stated educational goal of American public education, namely education for democratic citizenship. This chapter begins to explore this conflict, focusing on how the A Nation at Risk paradigm has curtailed students' and teachers' civic agency, a necessary aspect of democratic citizenship. The first part of the chapter explores the democratic aims of education first discussed in the previous chapters. As the history of student protests and teacher strikes demonstrates, education for democratic citizenship has a long tradition of being an aim of America's public schools. This section more fully explores its meaning, ideological roots, and the ways in which it has informed public education in the United States. Next, it turns to a discussion of how realizing the democratic aims of education requires schools to cultivate student and teachers' civic agency—a collection of traits, skills, and dispositions that are essential to democratic citizenship and that public education is uniquely positioned to develop.

The second part of the chapter offers a deeper understanding of the conservative modernization of American education and the A Nation at Risk paradigm, with an eye toward how these various beliefs and values have been translated into educational policy. The ideologies and policies that stem from this paradigm redefine democratic citizenship and impede the ability of public schools to cultivate student and teachers' civic agency. This analysis focuses on three domains of educational policy that impact the development of civic agency in schools. First, it explores the ways in which schools are organized, including their policies, procedures, and how they address student conduct. Next, it looks to the pedagogies and curricula of schools. Finally, it investigates the ways in which students and teachers are situated within the creation and implementation of educational policy. Since 1983, each of these domains has been impacted by the A Nation at Risk paradigm in important ways that operate to hinder the cultivation of student and teachers' civic agency. Given that the student and teacher civic activism of 2018 occurred nearly 35 years into this policy paradigm, understanding the ways in which the A Nation at Risk paradigm has impacted student and teacher civic agency will set the stage for understanding how these movements emerged, how they interrupt and challenge this paradigm, and how they offer the foundation for a new way forward.

DEMOCRATIC CITIZENSHIP AS AN AIM OF EDUCATION

Education for democratic citizenship has been—and continues to be—a dominant idea of American educational thought. As discussed during the history of student protests, there is a long history in the United States of democratic citizenship as an aim of education. From the Founding Fathers to the proponents of public commons schools in the 19th century, to the courts during the civil rights era, arguments for and recognition of the civic aims of public education have motivated educational policy throughout American history. Today, the idea that public education ought to prepare students for democratic citizenship is widely accepted, though how schools ought to prepare students for citizenship is often hotly contested. All 50 states require students to take some form of civics education (Koyama, 2017), but the extent to which our current schools realize the educational aim of democratic citizenship remains an open question.

In addition to having a firm historical and cultural foundation, democratic citizenship as an aim of education also has strong philosophical support in American intellectual thought. Gutmann (1987), relying on deliberative democratic theory, argues that education for citizenship is the only defensible justification for a nonneutral public education in a pluralistic, democratic society. While her argument does not preclude the pursuit of other aims of education, other aims are subordinate to the need to educate students for democratic participation. In making her argument, Gutmann addresses a fundamental tension in liberal democracies between majoritarian rule and individual rights or liberties. In pluralistic democratic societies, majoritarian control over public education results in an education that is nonneutral—as all education must be given its concern with the development of the person, a value-laden endeavor. Because educational policy resulting from majoritarian rule is informed by a convergence of different ideologies and beliefs about the good life, there are often conflicts between the policy prescriptions of majoritarian rule and the individual liberties of students, who are compelled to attend those schools, as well as their parents. The ideas of some students and their parents about the good life, and the ways in which education ought to promote it, will inevitably conflict with those of the majority.

Gutmann reasons that the only sufficient justification for allowing the majority to impose a nonneutral education on others, thereby infringing on their liberty interests, is if the nonneutral education prepares students to engage in the deliberative decision-making of majoritarian rule and the "conscious social reproduction" of society (p. 42). This neatly solves the dilemma of majoritarian rule versus individual liberty by ensuring that the loss of present liberty is limited by the need to ensure future liberty and the ability of students to be active participants in democratic life. To realize this end, Gutmann proposes a democratic threshold for the allocation of educational resources. This threshold "imposes a moral requirement that democratic institutions allocate sufficient resources to education to provide all children with an ability adequate to participate in the democratic process" (p. 136).

Where Gutmann's arguments rely on a preexisting democratic society that values deliberative processes and communal decision-making, John Dewey (1916/2012) argues for an education aimed at cultivating civic virtues based on his views of the nature of education and the benefits of democratic life. For Dewey, "the aim of education is to enable individuals to continue their education—or that the object and reward of learning is continued capacity for growth" (p. 100). Dewey, informed by the work and thinking of Ella Flagg Young (Blount, 2017), goes on to argue that democracy—like education—cultivates the capacity for individual growth due to the nature of democratic life as an associational, shared, and collaborative way of living where individuals must work together to realize both the common good and their individual interests. Because of this connection, Dewey argues that education for growth can only take place within a democratic society and that a democratic society requires an education that instills in children the traits, skills, and character necessary for democratic citizenship.

Taken together, the philosophical justifications for democratic citizenship as a proper aim of education in the United States, coupled with the practical concerns of historical figures like Thomas Jefferson, Benjamin Rush, and Chief Justice Earl Warren—the author of the Supreme Court's *Brown v. Board of Education* decision—offer compelling reasons to embrace democratic citizenship as an aim of education.

Democratic Citizenship and Civic Agency

In order to realize the democratic aims of education, public education must prepare students to practice democratic citizenship, which requires three interrelated capabilities. First, it requires individuals to be able to exercise cognitive autonomy (Newman, 2013). Citizens must have the intellectual flexibility necessary to engage with a variety of different values and ideas as well as the ability to evaluate and reflect on those ideas based on democratic values and an individual's sense of the common good (Ben-Porath, 2013). Cognitive autonomy also encompasses the possession of substantive knowledge—like foundational understandings of math, history, science, economics, and culture—that are necessary to understand, evaluate, and reflect on the social and political issues of the day (Newman, 2013).

Second, democratic citizenship entails the ability and willingness to engage in democratic deliberation based on public reason (Newman, 2013). The ability to engage in public reason requires both the rhetorical and listening skills necessary to make, listen to, and respond to arguments in the deliberative process as well as the ability to couch those arguments within mutually acceptable and justifiable terms. Democratic citizens must be able to engage in deliberative processes and understand which arguments will be successful within those spaces so that they can engage in the "conscious social reproduction" of society (Gutmann, 1987, p. 42).

Finally, democratic citizenship requires individuals to have dispositions toward tolerance, equality, and respect (Ben-Porath, 2013). They must be predisposed to accepting the pluralism of people, cultures, and ideas that are present in society and in deliberative processes. Democratic citizens must also be disposed to respect the equal rights of other citizens and their rights to engage in deliberative democracy (Hess & McAvoy, 2015).

Implicit within these three demands of democratic citizenship is a conception of the autonomous individual who is capable of acting to realize their goals and their conception of the common good. This has led many scholars to identify autonomy as a necessary element of democratic citizenship (e.g., Callan, 2000; Gutmann, 1987; Levinson, 1999). However, focusing exclusively on autonomy captures only half the picture.

Democratic citizens must not only be able to act reflectively and intelligently in pursuing their own ends; they must also be able to engage and work with others to pursue those ends and to navigate the collective pursuit of the common good. To put it another way, democratic citizens must be autonomous individuals who are able to exercise *civic agency*. They must possess the ability to make reasoned, considered decisions—individually and in deliberation with others—as they engage with and shape their social experience (Boyte & Finders, 2016). This conception of civic agency incorporates many of the aspects of cognitive autonomy and the ability to engage in public reason, and it directs those traits toward collaborative action in realizing the reproduction of society through democratic processes. Civic agency is thus understood as the ability to work with others to influence the world around us. Boyte and Finders (2016) call this the "public work" of citizenship (p. 130). In addition to the capacity to work with others to shape society, civic agency requires a sense of efficacy—a belief in one's equal membership in society and in their ability to act with and shape that society (Ben-Porath, 2013).

Ultimately, civic agency is a necessary but not sufficient aspect of democratic citizenship. Where democratic citizenship is focused on the rights, obligations, and privileges of citizens, civic agency focuses on the aspects of citizenship that are necessary to allow citizens to work with others to engage in democratic processes in order to influence their outcomes. Simply put, civic agency is the *how* of democratic citizenship. It is how individuals work with others in order to act on and shape society.

Public schools are in a privileged position for cultivating the civic agency necessary for democratic citizenship. First, civic agency and its underlying skills, knowledge, and dispositions are directly educable. A growing body of evidence suggests that direct instruction in civics and history leads to the development of civic virtues and practices (Delli-Carpini & Keeter, 1996; Nie et al., 1996; Niemi & Junn, 1998) and that there is a strong correlation between education and civic engagement (Dee, 2004, p. 1700). Second, mandatory schooling, whether through a public school, private school, or home schooling, is the primary social mechanism—outside the family—that our society relies on to prepare students for life. Like citizenship, it is perhaps one of the only inculcative experiences a vast majority of Americans will share, and it is therefore incumbent on schools to prepare students to be productive citizens.

However, today's schools face substantial obstacles to realizing the civic agency of students and teachers. The current dominant educational ideologies that inform the A Nation at Risk paradigm undermine the ability of schools to foster the sort of democratic citizenship and civic agency discussed. The next section discusses the A Nation at Risk paradigm and how it affects student and teacher civic agency.

THE A NATION AT RISK PARADIGM AND ITS IMPACTS ON STUDENT AND TEACHER CIVIC AGENCY

Within the A Nation at Risk paradigm, educational success is viewed as being central to national economic success, which has translated into the common belief that "American schools across the boards are substantially underperforming and in need of reform" (Mehta, 2013, p. 286). Mehta (2013) goes on to say:

> This paradigm has directed the school reform movement over the last 25 years, producing a variety of policy efforts that are consistent with its tenets, including charter schools, public school choice, vouchers, and . . . the growth of state and federal efforts to impose standards and introduce accountability. These assumptions not only have redirected the policy goals around schooling; they

have restructured the politics of education. Specifically, under the reign of the *A Nation at Risk* paradigm, more powerful political actors have entered the domain; interest groups have shifted to embrace the new paradigm; critics out of step with the paradigm have been rhetorically marginalized; and the venue in which education policy is discussed has shifted upwards, as the new paradigm has legitimized the claims of federal and state government to assert increasing control over what had previously been the province of local districts. (p. 286)

Under the A Nation at Risk paradigm, educational policy has become more highly centralized, democratic control has been displaced by a market vision of consumer control, and schools have become more tightly regulated and controlled. Each of these shifts, and the A Nation at Risk paradigm itself, rests on the ideological and political coalition of what Apple (2005) calls the "conservative modernization" of American education.

Apple (1988, 2005) argues that the conservative modernization of America's schools has been the result of a coalition of conservative ideologies that have reshaped educational policy—and that continue to dominate it (McGregor, 2018). Among this coalition are three broad groups, each with their own ideologies and policy goals: neoliberals, who see the free market as the most efficient allocator of resources and who view freedom in terms of individuals being able to make decisions in the free market; neoconservatives, who view the state as an appropriate vessel to promote conservative ideologies surrounding knowledge, values, and the body; and religious authoritarian populists, who seek to promote conservative "Christian morality" and who view pluralism in the public sphere as a threat to their religious truth (Apple, 2005).

Neoconservatives and religious authoritarian populists have had significant influence on the educational content of the school curriculum in recent decades (Apple, 2014), but neoliberalism has been the driving force in shaping the ways in which we think about education and teachers in this period of conservative modernization (Lipman, 2011). As Ball (2016) recognizes, "[Neoliberalism] change[s] what it means to be educated, what it means to teach and learn, what it means to be a teacher. [It] do[es] not just change what we do; [it] also change[s] who we are, how we think about what we do, how we relate to one another, how we decide what is important and what is acceptable, what is tolerable" (p. 1050).

Neoliberalism, as a political and economic ideology, is founded on the belief that competition in the free market is both the most efficient way to allocate goods and the best way to secure individual freedoms (Lipman, 2011). This leads neoliberalism to conflate democracy and global capitalism (Mirra & Morrell, 2011), which results in what Apple (2018) calls a "thin" version of democracy that replaces democratic deliberation with individual consumer choice. In practice, neoliberalism imposes the logic of the market into government. This finds expression in two ways: the privatization of public goods and services in the name of fostering open, competitive markets and the internalization of market logics and ideologies into government itself (Ball, 2016).

Education has been subject to both of these methods of marketization. Structurally, neoliberalism has led to the privatization of both the provision of education—through the proliferation of charter schools and calls for "school choice"—as well as the products used in education. However, under neoliberalism, school choice mechanisms often lead to the substitution of public schools with private schools that are less responsive to democratic control. This means that, while families have more control over which school their child will attend, they have less control over the governance of schools, including how their child will be educated and what their child will learn. Families become consumers of educational options rather than participants in their organization and governance. This also reinforces the second way in which schools have structurally been influenced by neoliberal marketization. With the proliferation of private and charter schools and accountability mechanisms based on standardized tests, for-profit management companies have increasingly become responsible for operating schools, and the content of education for all students has come to be dominated by private companies who are responsible for creating standardized tests and their associated curriculum.

Internally, neoliberalism has contributed to schools being retheorized as businesses. While schools in the United States have often been modeled on industrial metaphors in pursuit of efficiency, this shift influences beliefs about the role of education and what it means to be educated, which neoliberalism defines as the ability to be competitive in the global economy (Mirra & Morrell, 2011). Under neoliberalism, this goal is seen as the primary—and, in many ways, the only legitimate—goal of education. These shifts toward understanding schools as businesses serving the needs of the economy influence the relationships of students to schools, teachers to administrators and policymakers, and schools to communities (Allen, 2006). Ball (2016) describes these influences as the effects of management and performance, two highly interconnected methods employed by neoliberalism to "marketize" government.

Under neoliberalism, government structures like schooling shift from *government* by elected and democratically accountable bodies toward *governance*, characterized with control by experts who manage and direct decision-making about schools (Lipman, 2011). Hand-in-hand with the shift from government toward governance is neoliberalism's emphasis on accountability and performance. As neoliberalism embraces a managed-manager perspective, the managed—schools, teachers, and students—become more tightly controlled through accountability measures designed to evaluate their performances in meeting the goals and objectives prioritized by neoliberalism (Ball, 2016). While accountability is important, neoliberalism shifts what schools, teachers, and students are accountable for and to whom they are to be held accountable. These shifts have important implications for how schools develop and navigate student civic agency.

Neoliberalism, School Cultures, and the Crime Control Paradigm

Deriving from the rise of the A Nation at Risk paradigm and the ascendance of the conservative modernization, school cultures since the 1970s have become more rigidly controlled and increasingly defined by punishment and surveillance. Hirschfield and Celinska (2011) term this new order "the criminalization of school discipline." The criminalization of school discipline refers to more than just a shift toward punishing student misconduct as criminal offenses. Rather, it encompasses "the manner in which policymakers and school actors think and communicate about the problem of student rule-violation as well as myriad dimensions of school praxis including architecture, penal procedure, and security technology and tactics" (Hirschfield & Celinska, 2011, p. 80). Thus, the criminalization of school discipline marks a shift in the ways in which policymakers and school personnel think about and implement policies and practices surrounding school discipline. This shift has profound implications for student civic agency.

The crime control paradigm that dominates school cultures and mediates students' experiences within schools derives from the coalition of ideologies of the conservative modernization—neoliberalism, neoconservatism, and authoritarian populism. Inherent in neoconservatism is a desire for a return to traditional values and morality (Apple, 2005). One of the values in this constellation of traditional morality is the deference of children to adult, typically male, authority. Within this framework, students defer to legitimate authorities and embody the traditional values prioritized by neoconservatives. When they do not, this is seen as a direct threat to these legitimate authorities and has to be addressed in such a way that both affirms the punisher's authority over the student and deters the student from engaging in similar conduct. This ideology, then, justifies severe punishments of students in order to deter them from future bad behavior and grants significant and unrelenting authority to administrators and teachers who are tasked with policing and correcting student behavior. Both these phenomena can be seen in the shift of school discipline toward the crime control paradigm.

Similarly, neoliberalism has also contributed to the rise of the crime control paradigm in America's schools. First, neoliberalism, through the exacerbation of societal inequality and the centralization of political authority, requires greater mechanisms of social control to maintain social stability and state legitimacy (Simon, 2006). As Lipman (2011) argues, "Coercion is the other face of neoliberal governance . . . to manage the contradictions produced by neoliberalism, the state intensifies surveillance, punishment, and incarceration to maintain order in society" (p. 14). The intensification of surveillance, punishment, and incarceration has been mir-rored in schools (Hirschfield, 2008). Second, as neoliberal ideologies impose greater accountability measures on schools, educational policymakers have been incentivized to exclude "failing" students from schools and engender general compliance within the standardized testing regime (Fuentes, 2003). As will be discussed more fully later, accountability measures often result in a narrower and less relevant curriculum that is less engaging for students. Thus, criminalization policies assist schools in compelling compliance. As curricular and pedagogical shifts erode students' motivation to engage with schooling, the crime control paradigm has emerged as a new mechanism of control to ensure that students complete the tasks necessary for schools to be successful on the accountability measures that have been imposed on them.

Finally, drawing from social reconstruction theory (Bourdieu & Passeron, 1990), neoliberalism—as the dominant social ideology—has re-structured schools and schooling to prepare students to accept their roles within the highly stratified economic and social reality engendered by neo-liberalism (Hirschfield, 2008). Kupchik and Monahan (2006) describe the ways in which contemporary schools fulfill this role:

> The New American School facilitates the criminalization of poor students in or-der to establish and maintain a criminal class to legitimate systems of inequality in modern capitalist states. It rewards flexible students who can adapt or submit to labor instability, invasive monitoring and exploitative work conditions. It ac-commodates industry's desire for new markets by creating a demand for costly high-tech equipment that can only be provided by private companies, and can only be paid for, seemingly, with public funds. (p. 628)

In this context, the criminalization of schools prepares students for the reali-ties of the neoliberal state. It socializes some students to accept institutional-ized control and incarceration with the understanding that some individuals within the neoliberal state are conceived of as surplus laborers who occupy geographic locations that are more productive for capital accumulation when put to other uses. Students are also prepared to accept external au-thority that is not responsive to individual voice or context, and students are taught to expect constant monitoring and surveillance. Ultimately, under neoliberalism and the crime control paradigm, students are stratified through credentialing, criminalization, and other mechanisms to assume po-sitions within the economy. And schools do all of this while also implicitly socializing students to accept the larger neoliberal social order.

At the federal level, the crime control paradigm began with a 1978 report by the National Institute of Education entitled "Violent Schools—Safe Schools: The Safe School Study Report to Congress." The Safe School Study was the first national study of school crime in the United States. With

$2.4 million in funding, the National Institute of Education (1978) surveyed over 4,000 public schools; conducted studies of nearly 650 junior high and high schools; engaged in thousands of interviews of students, teachers, and school administrators; and employed 10 in-depth case studies of schools that had successfully reduced the incidence of crime on their campuses. After its exhaustive data collection, the National Institute of Education concluded that America's schools were plagued by drug and crime problems.

To address this, the Safe School Study outlined two sets of recommendations for Congress. The first set of recommendations was student focused. It called for understanding why students commit crime and for addressing the underlying causes of crime and disobedience in schools by reducing school and class sizes, giving students more voice and agency, removing subjective rules to promote fairness and equality, and overhauling the school curriculum to be more relevant to students' lives. The other set of recommendations focused on controlling crime rather than preventing it. These proposals called for increases in the use of security technology in schools, including greater surveillance of students and harsher penalties for wrongdoing. Congress and the courts ultimately embraced the second set of recommendations, helping give rise to the criminalization of school discipline.

In the 1990s, Congress adopted two significant pieces of legislation addressing issues of school discipline that further operationalized the criminalization of school discipline. First, in 1994, Congress passed the Safe and Drug Free Schools Act, which provided millions in grant dollars to schools seeking to develop partnerships with community organizations to prevent and address crime and drug use. While the Safe and Drug Free School Act may have focused primarily on preventing violence and drug use through community partnerships, it further exacerbated the idea of the school as a criminalized space—the title itself assumes that schools are not currently drug or violence free—and set the stage for more punitive forays by Congress into school discipline, as demonstrated by another 1994 act, the Gun-Free Schools Act. The Gun-Free Schools Act compelled schools to adopt policies that required students who possessed firearms on school grounds to be expelled. Schools that failed to adopt such policies would have their federal funds withheld. This act imposed a national zero-tolerance policy for gun possession on school campuses and set the stage for state expansion of zero-tolerance policies for other types of infractions (Black, 2016). Both these acts by Congress grew out of the "Violent Schools—Safe Schools" study and demonstrate the emerging understanding of the school as a criminalized space.

In addition to Congressional action, the crime control paradigm found expression in significant U.S. Supreme Court decisions that limited students' rights in schools as related to school discipline. In 1985, the Court held that, while students have Fourth Amendment rights to be free from unreasonable searches and seizures in schools, those rights are limited by the school context (*New Jersey v. T.L.O.*, 1985). Citing the "Violent Schools—Safe Schools" report, the Court relied in part on the image of the school as a dangerous space in upholding the warrantless search of a student's purse for contraband. The Court held that students in schools may be searched by school officials so long as the officials have a reasonable suspicion of wrongdoing and the search is not overly intrusive given the context, a substantially relaxed standard compared to general Fourth Amendment warrant requirements applicable to law enforcement officers. Further limiting student rights in schools, in a pair of cases, *Vernonia v. Acton* (1995) and *Board of Education v. Earls* (2002), the Court upheld suspicionless, random drug testing of students engaged in extracurricular activities. The Court again relied on ideas of schools as criminalized spaces to hold that the school's interest in preventing illegal drug use outweighed the intrusion into students' protected privacy interests. Ultimately, these decisions were predicated on shifting understandings of schools as criminalized spaces and facilitated this transition by curtailing students' rights in schools.

The trend to criminalize school discipline has also found expression at the state level. At the most extreme end of the spectrum, a number of state and local school boards have voted to transfer responsibility for school safety to local law enforcement agencies, fully turning these schools into policed spaces (Magee, 2001). Less extreme examples include state laws increasing penalties for crimes committed on school grounds, states mandating that schools report crime to local law enforcement agencies, and zero-tolerance policies for often trivial forms of student misconduct (Beger, 2002).

Translated into policy and practice at the federal, state, and local level, the crime control paradigm is characterized by stricter control of student bodies, an increase in punitive punishments like exclusionary discipline and zero-tolerance policies, increased surveillance of students, and the growing presence of police in schools (Black, 2016). Closely mirroring the rise of the criminalization of schools, the usage of exclusionary discipline has exploded since the 1970s. Between 1974 and 1998, the rates of school suspensions and expulsions nearly doubled (Schiraldi & Ziedenberg, 2001). In the 2011–2012 school year alone, 3.5 million students were given in-school suspensions, nearly 3.5 million were given one or more out-of-school suspensions, and 130,000 students were expelled from school altogether (Office for Civil Rights, U.S. Department of Education, 2014). Importantly, the rise in the use of exclusionary discipline does not correspond to an increase in student misbehavior or juvenile delinquency, suggesting that students in schools are being punished more harshly for similar or even less problematic conduct (Fabelo et al., 2011; Schiraldi & Ziedenberg, 2001; Skiba & Rausch, 2006).

Another way that the criminalization of schools finds expression in policy is through the increase in surveillance technology and practices employed by schools to monitor students. Modern schools use a variety of methods and technologies to observe students and monitor their activities. One common set of policies is to control and monitor access to the school building for both students and the public. For example, recent studies have shown that 96% of schools require guests to sign in before entering the school, approximately 85% of schools lock and monitor their doors, and 80% have closed campus policies that require students to not leave the building during the school day (Dinkes et al., 2007; Gegax et al., 1998). Another common set of policies is to employ technology to monitor and record student activity. Dinkes et al. (2007) found that nearly 70% of all public schools in the United States use security cameras. This is a marked increase from 1999 when only 19% of schools used them (Brent, 2016, p. 522). In addition to monitoring and controlling access to the school environment, schools also employ a variety of practices to search students and monitor their possessions and activities. For example, Dinkes et al. (2007) found that 60% of schools used drug-sniffing dogs to perform sweep searches of students and their belongings, 30% performed random sweeps of lockers and other student possessions for contraband, 12.7% required student athletes to submit to drug testing, and 11% used metal detectors.

The final and perhaps most significant manifestation of the criminalization of schools is the increased presence of law enforcement officers on school grounds. Prior to 1975, only 1% of school principals reported having a police officer stationed in their school (National Institute of Education, 1978). Approximately 20 years later, in the 1996–1997 school year, the 1st year in which national data was collected on the presence of police in schools, there were 9,446 police officers assigned to public schools in the United States and about 19% of all schools had an officer assigned full-time (Beger, 2002, pp. 121–122). In 2010, the total number of police officers in schools had increased to as many as 17,000 (Wald & Thurau, 2010) and, by the 2013–2014 school year, 41% of all schools reported having a police officer stationed in the school for either all or part of the school day (NCES, 2015). These numbers have continued to increase due in part to federal funding from the Office of Community Oriented Policing Services (COPS), which has contributed $905 million to local communities to assist in hiring over 6,300 school resource officers (Justice Policy Institute, 2011).

In many ways, the crime control paradigm is antithetical to the development of student civic agency. It transforms an environment in which students already have limited voice and authority (Goodman, 2010) to one in which students have no voice or authority, which are important elements of civic agency. It cultivates feelings of powerlessness, negative attitudes toward schooling, and an individualized self-protective posture (Mullet, 2014). If civic agency requires students to be able to both engage with others to shape their social experiences and believe in their ability to do so, the crime control paradigm directly impedes their development of these traits. As Ben-Porath (2013) writes:

> [T]he morality—or the attendant values—of the ensuing [totalizing schools] are such that they prohibit the development of an active moral (or other) community, and thus they fail to contribute to the education of students as citizens and in particular to their ability to develop the kind of agency, self-perception and relationships that support the development of civic virtues. . . . As a result, self-reflection is hardly possible, and personal or social relations are minimized. Self-reflection is limited to asking, "have I made a good choice?," which directly translates to "have I followed the rules?" There is therefore little opportunity for children and young people to develop interests, views, perceptions of self and others, or ideas about desired and desirable actions. . . . The opportunity to develop agency, to learn to see oneself as a contributing member of society, to understand oneself relationally in positive terms, these are all minimized by the strict controls and limited, structured interaction and forms of expression in totalizing schools. (pp. 122–123)

By socializing students to external control, subjecting them to constant and intrusive surveillance, and harshly punishing them when they violate rules and norms that they did not participate in creating, schools characterized by the crime control paradigm communicate to students that they are the passive recipients of external authority. Not only does this paradigm deny students opportunities to develop and practice civic agency, but this message is in direct opposition to the goal of fostering their democratic citizenship. Instead of being encouraged to be active civic agents, students become passive objects of policy, which has profound implications for their development of civic agency and their future relationship with the state as democratic citizens.

Pedagogy and Curriculum: Accountability and Student and Teacher Civic Agency

Like the crime control paradigm, the A Nation at Risk paradigm's focus on accountability and economic productivity also has significant consequences for the development of student and teacher civic agency. Accountability is a key feature of the paradigm and aligns with the ways in which neoliberalism reshapes relationships toward managed–manager associations (Ball, 2016). This finds expression in educational policy through the proliferation of standardized tests, the development of state and national curriculum aligned with those tests, and mechanisms that connect funding and employment decisions to their results. Importantly, these high-stakes testing regimes are a mechanism of neoliberalism and are informed by the ideologies of the conservative modernization. This means that these testing regimes (1) prioritize the economic skills necessary for students to be productive members of the national economy and (2) emphasize "the revivification of the 'Western tradition,' patriotism, and conservative variants of character education" because of the ways neoconservatism promotes conservative values and beliefs (Apple, 2005, p. 279).

Perhaps the most significant example of school accountability being put into practice under the A Nation at Risk paradigm is the federal No Child Left Behind Act (NCLB) of 2001. The stated goal of NCLB was to narrow the achievement gaps between different subgroups within America's schools. Consistent educational data demonstrated that poor students and minority students chronically underperformed compared to their affluent or majority peers. To accomplish this goal, NCLB operationalized accountability of schools at the federal level by requiring all schools receiving federal funds to test all students on math and reading in grades 3 through 8 and once in high school (Ravitch, 2010). Under NCLB, states were given flexibility in choosing their tests and required performance levels, with the understanding that all states would achieve 100% proficiency for all students by 2014, with each state defining "proficiency" for itself. Student scores on these standardized tests were aggregated based on subgroups, and schools that failed to meet "adequate yearly progress" (AYP) for any subgroup were subjected to sanctions that became increasing burdensome after each consecutive year. Schools that failed to meet AYP after 1 year were put on notice. After 5 years of failing to meet AYP, schools were required to completely restructure, convert to a charter school, or be turned over to the state or a private management company. While NCLB was reauthorized as the Every Student Succeeds Act in 2015 and many of its more burdensome requirements have been eliminated, the high-stakes testing regime that it endorsed still has important ramifications for schools today, especially related to student and teacher civic agency.

Like NCLB, the nationwide push for states to adopt the Common Core State Standards is another significant manifestation of the accountability strands of the A Nation at Risk paradigm. Developed by a consortium of private foundations, corporations, and governmental groups at the behest of the National Governors Association and the Council of Chief State School Officers, the Common Core consists of English language arts and math standards for grades K–12. The stated goal of the standards is to ensure students' "college and career readiness." The standards make a single reference to preparation for "private deliberation and responsible citizenship in a republic," but this statement is found on the third and final page of the introduction to the standards (Neem, 2018).

While adoption of the Common Core was never mandated by the federal government, President Obama incentivized states to adopt the standards through the Race to the Top program. Under Race to the Top, states and districts applied to the government to receive educational grants that were allocated based on the applicant's adherence to the administration's policy priorities, which included the adoption of the Common Core. By 2013, 45 states had adopted the Common Core. However, due to political conflict over the local control of education and the role of the federal government in making local educational decisions, some states have since replaced or modified the standards. By shifting educational policy decisions toward centralized governmental bodies and private entities and by prioritizing the economic rather than the civic goals of education, the Common Core is in many ways a manifestation of the A Nation at Risk paradigm.

The accountability regime—expressed through policies like NCLB and the Common Core—erodes and constrains student and teacher civic agency. By reorienting the curriculum toward economic considerations, the accountability regime has contributed to a reframing of popular understandings of agency, autonomy, and citizenship. Within this paradigm, informed by neoliberal ideologies, students are educated for employment, consumerism, and a version of citizenship that conflates public life with the private consumption of government goods. Each of these trends distorts civic agency. While capacity for productive employment is certainly an important aspect of democratic citizenship in a capitalist, liberal democracy, rampant consumerism flips the script on autonomy and civic agency. Impulsive consumption is privileged over thoughtful self-regulation, desires are directed away from the public good and toward the goods of private producers, and passive consumption crowds out active social reproduction (Schinkel et al., 2010). Neoliberalism also perverts civic agency by privatizing government and reframing citizens as consumers:

> As collective responsibility is privatized, politics loses its social and democratic character. The formative culture necessary for the production of engaged critical agents is gravely undermined. An utterly reduced form of agency is now embodied in the figure of the isolated automaton driven by self-interest and eschewing any responsibility for the other. (Giroux, 2013, p. 517)

Thus, not only does the conservative modernization reduce the agency of teachers and students through accountability mechanisms, it also reframes what those concepts come to mean.

In addition, the accountability regime, by connecting significant adverse outcomes to how well schools perform on standardized tests, has resulted in a narrowing of the curriculum that has led many schools to neglect civics education and has contributed to many students disengaging from schooling. As schools are held accountable for student achievement, they naturally focus their attention on the areas that are being measured. Further compounding this issue is the rise of the education services sector, which consists of for-profit publishers and test-makers who both create the standardized tests and market curricula to schools that are narrowly focused on improving scores on those tests (Sloan, 2008). The results of this are that schools in the age of accountability often focus disproportionate time and resources on math and reading instruction—the focus of NCLB and the Common Core—to the detriment of science, history, social studies, physical education, and the arts (Ravitch, 2010). As discussed, math and reading are important aspects of the knowledge necessary for democratic citizenship but not to the exclusion of other vital knowledge and skills.

By focusing significant attention on the subjects tested by standardized tests, schools not only neglect other subject areas important for the cultivation of civic agency, but the resulting tightening of control and the loss of other areas of interest to students means that students are less motivated at school and have less autonomy within the classroom (Curren, 2014). This leads to a vicious cycle as students, disengaged by the constant test prep and narrow curricular focus, require greater and greater mechanisms of control to coerce them into the learning necessary to do well on standardized tests, further denying their agency and eroding their motivation (Pelletier & Sharp, 2009).

This narrowing of the curriculum also has important implications for teacher agency. As states and schools adopt state and national content standards—along with the commercial curricula that align with them and the standardized tests that measure them—teachers lose their professional autonomy to develop their own curriculum. Instead, they become compliance operatives responsible for faithfully implementing the formal curriculum (Spina, 2017). This not only limits the ways in which teachers can direct the curriculum toward values, knowledge, and dispositions not valued within the A Nation at Risk paradigm, but also denies teachers the ability to exercise their civic agency as they are denied any participation in the creation of the curriculum or in how it is implemented.

Finally, even where civic education is addressed within the narrowed curriculum, the accountability regime often focuses such education on quantifiable information and knowledge rather than the skills, traits, and dispositions of civic agency. As Koyama (2017) writes, contemporary civics education "stresses teaching students a common body of knowledge about U.S. history and government structures[, but] the content and pedagogy of civic education in school is often disconnected from contemporary issues relevant in students' lives" (p. 3). Thus, students learn about *government*, but they don't learn the skills, traits, and dispositions necessary for *governing*. Such an education is uncritical about what citizenship requires in a democratic society and does not provide students with opportunities to meaningfully explore and develop their civic agency (Metzger, 2002).

Ultimately, the accountability regime "displace[s] the agency of the educators, students, and communities that know their children best" (Boyte & Finders, 2016, p. 136). As discussed next, this also has important implications for the role that students and teachers play within school governance and educational policy.

School Governance and the Positioning of Students and Teachers Within Educational Policy

The A Nation at Risk paradigm has substantially shifted the ways in which America's schools are organized and governed. Henig (2013) identifies three fault lines in American educational policy around issues of school governance: public sector versus private sector, centralization versus decentralization, and single-purpose versus general-purpose governance. Within this paradigm, the private wins out over the public, educational policy becomes more centralized, and school governance is both privatized and shifted away from single-purpose governing bodies, like school boards, and toward general-purpose government bodies, like state legislators, governors, and even courts. These shifts find expression in the proliferation of school voucher programs, charter schools, private management companies, state-led management of distressed school districts, mayoral and gubernatorial takeovers of educational policy domains, and the elevation of educational policy decisions to higher and less-responsive governing bodies or to private entities with little or no democratic oversight. Taken together, these shifts have profound impacts on student and teacher civic agency both within schools and within educational policy (Anderson & Cohen, 2018).

For teachers, these shifts have limited the ability of teachers to impact decisions surrounding the organization and governance of schools, positioning teachers as passive recipients of educational policy. Further, the centralization and elevation of educational policy has eroded the political power of teachers' unions and allowed other interest groups to dominate policymaking decisions around education. Historically, teachers' unions have been powerful local interest groups in influencing educational policy. However, as policy decisions have moved further away from local schools, the relative power of teachers' unions has diminished as other powerful interest groups, like businesses and other advocacy groups, are also engaged in influencing educational policy. This phenomenon coupled with eroding legal protections for public unions—predicated on neoliberalism's assault on public organizations—has greatly weakened the civic agency of teachers as their ability to collectively impact educational policy has declined.

In addition to the weakening of teachers' civic agency due to the results of the A Nation at Risk paradigm, teachers are positioned within this paradigm in ways that deny their civic agency. Mirra and Morrell (2011) argue that neoliberalism positions the "teacher as conduit" (p. 409). Under this view, teachers are seen as conduits that transfer externally created, objective knowledge to their students. This mechanistic version of teaching positions teachers as passive recipients of policy whose value is derived from how well they are able to transfer knowledge—particularly the knowledge valued by neoliberalism and neoconservatism—to their students. In effect, this view of teachers embraces the "banking" concept of teaching outlined by Freire

(1970), which, Freire argues, denies teachers and students their agency and further perpetuates systems of oppression and domination.

Similarly, Boyte and Finders (2016) argue that standardization and high-stakes accountability measures have resulted in "shrinking agency for teachers" (p. 135). Because teachers are viewed as the transmitters of official knowledge and find themselves in more tightly controlled manager–managed relationships due to neoliberalism's dual emphasis on management and performance, teachers have limited discretion and agency under neoliberalism (Fisher-Ari et al., 2017). This finds expression in neoliberalism's view of teachers as "compliant operatives," technicians who are responsible for delivering the agendas of policy elites (Hall & McGinity, 2015, pp. 4–5). It also limits the proper scope of teachers' authority and responsibility such that teachers are unable to participate in the creation of educational policy (Anderson & Cohen, 2018). They become understood—and come to understand themselves—as compliers with policy rather than policymakers (Hinnant-Crawford, 2016).

Even this repositioning of teachers as passive compliers with policy, though, fails to fully grapple with the ways in which teachers are impacted by the larger policy projects of the A Nation at Risk paradigm. Neoliberalism, in its desire to privatize public goods and shrink the activities the government may legitimately pursue, often results in disinvestment in public goods, like schools. For education, this means that funding for public schools is either redirected to other education providers, typically to charter schools through school choice programs or to private schools through vouchers, or they are denied to the government altogether in the form of tax cuts that reduce governmental revenues. These impacts, when understood alongside neoliberalism's emphasis on management and performance, in which teachers are held solely responsible for their students' learning, lead teachers to be seen as martyrs who are required to sacrifice their own well-being for that of their students.

Neoliberalism's emphasis on management and performance heaps responsibility and culpability for student success and well-being on teachers while its emphasis on privatization and disinvestment in public goods leaves teachers with fewer resources and lower pay. This confluence results in teachers being asked to do more with less. Further, neoliberalism constrains the proper scope of teachers' activities such that they are powerless to speak back to this phenomenon through the erosion of their civic agency. Ultimately, then, teachers are held hostage by their responsibilities to their students and are forced to accept the larger impacts of the A Nation at Risk paradigm on education. Under the paradigm, then, teachers are passive policy compliers; but they are also "passive policy martyrs," expected to sacrifice themselves for the good of their students.

This positioning of teachers also complicates the ways in which schools are able to cultivate students' civic agency. Teachers are often viewed as role models for students. They model the traits, values, and dispositions that our educational system seeks to cultivate in its students. This is one reason denying teachers' civic agency is so insidious: Under the A Nation at Risk paradigm, the very people who ought to be modeling civic agency for students are unable to do so. At best, this is an unfortunate disconnect between public education's goal of cultivating democratic citizenship and the ways in which the paradigm positions teachers. At worst, it impedes the ability of students to develop their own civic agency, as those they look to for guidance are unable to lead by example.

In addition to teachers being unable to model civic agency for students under this paradigm, there is also reason to believe that increased accountability and tighter manager–managed relationships between teachers and administrators lead to teachers being less democratic and caring in their teaching (Ball, 2016). Thus, the way in which teachers are positioned within educational policy not only provides students with less than ideal models of civic agency but also impedes the cultivation of that agency through the educational process.

The A Nation at Risk paradigm positions students, like their teachers, as passive recipients of educational policy. As discussed with respect to the criminalizing of school discipline, the message that students receive in schools under this paradigm is to comply with policies rather than participate in their formation. Students within this paradigm are acted on rather than acted with. While the ability of students to influence educational policy has always been murky throughout American history, this paradigm has made it more difficult with the imposition of strict command and control policies and a corresponding limitation of students' rights.

Since 1969, the Supreme Court has repeatedly ruled in ways that limit student expressive rights in schools, with the notable exception of *Mahanoy Area School District v. B.L.* (2021), which dealt with school authority to regulate off-campus student speech. Following *Tinker v. Des Moines* (1969), in which the Supreme Court held that students enjoy First Amendment expressive rights in schools, subsequent cases have eroded those protections, often in ways that echo the ideologies informing the A Nation at Risk paradigm. *Tinker* marks the high-water mark for student expressive rights in schools. At issue in *Tinker* was a school's decision to suspend students for wearing black armbands to school in protest of the Vietnam War. In overturning the suspensions, the Supreme Court held that student expression could only be censored in schools if it either infringed on the rights of others or substantially interfered with the school's educational mission. However, subsequent cases have created broad exceptions to this rule. In *Bethel School District v. Fraser* (1986), the Supreme Court held that a student could be disciplined for delivering a sexually suggestive speech at a school assembly. Echoing neoconservative ideas about the proper content of school curriculum, the Court reasoned that such a speech could be curtailed because of a school's role in inculcating community values and cultivating appropriate behavior.

The Supreme Court came to a similar decision in *Hazelwood School District v. Kuhlmeier* (1988). Relying on the school's authority to pursue its educational mission, the Court rejected the claim of student journalists that their principal's censorship of their newspaper articles violated the First Amendment. This again echoes neoconservative ideas about the proper content of America's schools—the censored articles explored student experiences with their parents' divorces and teenage pregnancy—and reinforces neoliberalism's shift of educational authority toward educational experts. Then, in *Morse v. Frederick* (2007), the Supreme Court upheld the suspension of a student who unfurled a banner that read "Bong Hits 4 Jesus" at a school-sponsored event. In this case, the Court carved out another exception to *Tinker*, in which schools may censor student speech if it promotes drugs or other illegal activity. This aligns closely with the erosion of students' rights stemming from the criminalization of schools during the A Nation at Risk era. Indeed, the Court cited as its primary support for its rulings the challenges schools face with illegal drug use and its own precedent that limited students' rights to be free from unreasonable searches at school, decisions that were themselves informed by the criminalization of school discipline.

Because of this erosion in student expressive rights in schools and the ways that students are positioned within schools and educational policy, the ability of students to participate in the governance of their schools has been substantially curtailed by the A Nation at Risk paradigm, leading to a constriction of both teacher and student civic agency. Ultimately, under this paradigm, students are taught a curriculum that fails to fully prepare them for democratic citizenship by teachers who are unable to model that citizenship and who are compelled to teach in undemocratic ways. Students are thus denied the ability to develop their civic agency during their years of compulsory education, which for many of them will be their most significant personal relationship with the state. Instead of participating in the self-governance of schools, the A Nation at Risk paradigm positions students as the consumers—or even the products—of education.

Taken together, the impacts of the A Nation at Risk paradigm on student and teacher agency are profound. While America's schools have always grappled with how to balance economic and democratic influences in education—often prioritizing economic values and aims over democratic ones (Callahan, 1964; Haley, 2006)—the paradigm since 1983 has fundamentally changed education in the United States as it has injected market ideologies into educational policy and altered societal conceptions of citizenship. These shifts make the student protests and teacher strikes since the spring of 2018 that much more remarkable. The students and teachers engaged in those protests were not only protesting the outcomes of the A Nation at Risk paradigm; they were also exercising their civic agency from within an educational policy climate that actively redefines and discourages that agency. The next chapter explores this tension. Combining the lessons of the history of student and teacher civic activism with the impacts that this paradigm has had on their civic agency, it explores the ways in which these protests respond to and challenge the A Nation at Risk paradigm.

CHAPTER 5

Understanding Student Protests and Teacher Strikes at the Intersection of the A Nation at Risk Paradigm and the History of Student and Teacher Civic Activism

The student protests and teacher strikes during the spring of 2018 are part of a much larger history of activism, yet they occurred within a political environment that redefines, discourages, and is often actively hostile to student and teacher civic agency. The A Nation at Risk paradigm that has dominated educational policy during the past 30 years seeks to prevent students and teachers from gaining and exercising the skills, traits, and dispositions that are necessary for collective action. So how then should we understand this civic activism at the intersection of these two traditions? Building from their strong historical traditions, these student protests and teacher strikes constitute a rejection of the A Nation at Risk paradigm in at least three important ways. First, the students and teachers were reacting to and rejecting what the participants experienced as the untenable results of this paradigm. Students in the spring of 2018 were protesting against gun violence and the threat of guns in America's schools, including the impacts this has had on understandings of school as criminalized spaces. Gun rights and the unfettered individual right to bear arms have been firm staples of conservative politics during the conservative modernization. Similarly, the teacher strikes occurred in predominately conservative states where decades of the paradigm's policies had led to steep cuts in education funding and teacher compensation.

In addition to challenging the policy outcomes of the conservative modernization, the student and teacher civic activism of 2018 was also a rejection of the ways in which the A Nation at Risk paradigm positions students and teachers within educational policy. Similar to the 1960s and '70s, America in the 2000s and 2010s was marked by widespread civic protests such as Occupy Wall Street, the Tea Party, Black Lives Matter, and the

Women's March, among others (Jaffe, 2016). In their own ways, each of these protest movements was a reaction to neoliberalism and its tendency to consolidate political power with elites while at the same time redefining what civic agency is and how it can be exercised. For example, the Occupy Wall Street movement of 2011 was a rejection of increased wealth concentration in economic elites, which has been accelerated under neoliberal policies. In addition, though, the Occupy Wall Street movement also embraced democratic deliberation within public spaces to achieve a participatory consensus-based democracy, utilizing strategies such as talking circles and a movement-wide general assembly (Min, 2015). In this way, the Occupy movement was both a rejection of neoliberalism's policy outcomes and the ways in which it reorients civic agency and citizenship away from democratic participation and toward economic participation. Following in this tradition, the student and teacher protesters of 2018 also rejected not only the policy results of the A Nation at Risk paradigm but also how it positions them within educational policy.

Finally, these protests were fostered within and made possible through liminal shadow spaces and the ways in which the A Nation at Risk paradigm has organized the politics of education. "Shadow spaces" refer to communities or places "that stand apart from the glare of mainstream policy . . . where people have an important measure of room for self-organizing initiative, free from dominant cultural, social, and economic powers" (Boyte & Finders, 2016, p. 141). Within these shadow spaces that existed outside the paradigm, individuals and groups were able to come together to develop their civic agency and create coalitions for broader societal change (Polletta, 1999). For the students of Parkland, their shadow spaces were constituted by empowering school curricula, passionate teachers who emphasized the traits and skills of civic agency against countervailing political pressures, and social media—a platform that the Parkland students and other young people used to great avail in organizing and mobilizing the three nationwide student protests (Falkowski & Garner, 2018; Hogg & Hogg, 2018; March for Our Lives, 2018). For the teachers, their shadow spaces existed within both the traditional spaces of teacher unions—who are often the target of the A Nation at Risk paradigm and who often stand in opposition to it—as well as outside of them through social media and loose networks of social activism unconnected to traditional teacher unions.

In addition to these nourishing shadow spaces, both the student and teacher movements grew to reorganize the ways in which the A Nation at Risk paradigm has shaped the political landscape of educational policy. As Mehta (2013) argues, this paradigm operates to restructure the politics of education, limiting the legitimate participants within educational policy and ossifying its debates and battlelines in ways that are consistent with the paradigm's tenets. The students and teachers of 2018 broke free from these constraints. For student activists, they injected the missing and excluded voices of students into educational policy debates writ large, especially around issues related to gun violence and how it has impacted their lives at school. For teachers, they realigned teacher collective action toward centralized policymakers rather than local school districts. Following the 1970s, teachers' unions—which often, though not exclusively, represent the collective power of teachers—had largely directed their efforts at local school districts and toward obtaining formal legal protections and benefits for their members. The 2018 teacher strikes disrupted this pattern. Instead of being directed at local school districts, the teacher activists of 2018 directed their collective voice at their state governments, focusing on issues in education that involved more than just teacher compensation and their legal rights. While the teacher activists were often allied with existing teacher unions, they also organized outside those unions and pushed them into direct action against state governments, a path that existing teachers unions might not have otherwise taken.

Together, the long history of student protests and teacher strikes collided with the A Nation at Risk paradigm to inform the student and teacher civic activism of the spring of 2018. In the face of the paradigm's work in redefining student and teacher civic agency and impeding their civic participation, these activities constitute important rejections of the A Nation at Risk paradigm and its impacts on educational policy. However, whether these protests truly constitute a sea change in our current policy paradigm will be determined by the ways in which school officials and policymakers respond to these activities and how they embrace and expand the shadow spaces that foster them. This response will determine whether these activities are merely a blip within the A Nation at Risk paradigm or whether a new policy paradigm, grounded in student and teacher civic agency, will rise to challenge it.

THE IMPROBABLE PROTESTS: STUDENT AND TEACHER ACTIVISM AT THE INTERSECTION OF TWO CONFLICTING TRADITIONS

The student and teacher civic activism of 2018 occurred despite the A Nation at Risk paradigm. This paradigm, over the past 30 years, has continued to ossify policies and practices that redefine citizenship and deny students and teachers their civic agency. And yet, the 2018 protests continued a long history of student and teacher civic activism that celebrates and closely aligns with traditions of the democratic aims of education in the United States. Stemming back to the late 1800s for public primary and secondary students and the early 1900s for teachers, students and teachers have been engaged in civic protest for much of America's history. Again and again, they have each protested against policies that have deeply impacted their experiences in schools and have collectively advocated to improve their respective positions. These protests were understood within larger societal traditions, including those of labor and civic organizations of the times, and were also understood as aligning with the democratic aims of education in America.

Throughout American history, one of the primary purposes of education and one of its formative ideologies has been the desire to prepare students for participation in our democratic society. Civic agency, the ability to work with and alongside others in order to pursue individual goals and collective self-governance through the democratic process, is a necessary aspect of democratic citizenship, and the history of student and teacher civic activism is rife with student and teachers practicing their civic agency. The students and teachers of 2018 were enacting and celebrating this civic agency, but they were doing so within a policy paradigm that rejects such agency. Thus, to fully understand the importance of student protests and teacher strikes, it is necessary to understand how these protests interact with these two conflicting social traditions. To begin this work, I explored contemporary accounts of these student protests and teacher strikes from both popular media and the participants themselves. Together, their accounts tell the story of how they drew support from the strong traditions of student and teacher civic activism in the United States to speak back to and reject the outcomes of the A Nation at Risk paradigm.

Rejecting the Policy Outcomes of the A Nation at Risk Paradigm

The student and teacher activists of the spring of 2018 were reacting to a constellation of policy outcomes and proposals that found their genesis in the A Nation at Risk paradigm. Teachers during the wave of statewide teacher strikes were largely protesting against low teacher compensation, including reductions in health care coverage and rising health care costs, and poor working and learning conditions. In the first statewide teacher strike of 2018, West Virginian teachers were protesting rising health care costs, pro-charter legislation, proposed legislation that would have limited the political power of teacher unions, and low pay for public employees. In the next wave of teacher strikes, Kentucky's teachers were protesting the privatization of teacher pensions and the rising costs of health care, and Oklahoma's teachers engaged in a 9-day strike in pursuit of higher teacher compensation and greater investments in education. In the last wave of protests, Arizona, Colorado, and North Carolina's teachers were also seeking increased salaries for public employees, including school support staff and greater spending on education. All these protests can be read as responses to the policy outcomes of the A Nation at Risk paradigm.

All six states that experienced widespread teacher protests directed at the state level had an average teacher salary in 2018 that fell below the national average of $60,483 (NEA, 2018). Kentucky, the state with the highest teacher compensation of the six, ranked 30th out of the 50 states and the

District of Columbia, with an average teacher salary of $52,952. Colorado and North Carolina were close behind at 32nd and 37th nationally, while Arizona (46th), Oklahoma (49th), and West Virginia (50th)—the three states that experienced the most sustained and widespread teacher strikes— fell at the bottom with average salaries of $47,746, $45,678, and $45,642, respectively (NEA, 2018). Importantly, while these average salaries are low compared to other states, each of these states had also experienced a net decline in average teacher salaries since 2009, when adjusted for inflation. Teachers in these states were making less than they had in 2009, with reductions of 4.5% in Kentucky, 6.7% in Colorado, 9.4% in North Carolina, 10.1% in Oklahoma, 11% in Arizona, and 11.8% in West Virginia (NEA, 2018).

The teachers in these six states experienced salaries below the national average, but the disparity is compounded by the fact that teacher salaries nationwide are also relatively low compared to other professions. Nationwide, teacher compensation has fallen by 4% since 2009 (NEA, 2018). Compared to other professions, teachers typically make between 20–30% less than similarly educated individuals. This has led to roughly 1 in 5 teachers working a second job during the school year and a nationwide teacher shortage that has resulted in some 100,000 teaching positions being filled by unqualified instructors (Blanc, 2019). The teacher protests of 2018 were responding to both the relative compensation of teachers in each state and the disconnect between what teachers are paid and what teachers believe their work is worth.

In addition to protesting low teacher compensation, teachers were also protesting systemic underinvestment and disinvestment in educational spending. Like teacher salary, the majority of the states that experienced teacher strikes in 2018 fell below the national average in per-pupil expenditures, with West Virginia being the notable exception (NEA, 2018). Indeed, Oklahoma and Arizona ranked 45th and 48th, respectively, in per-pupil expenditures, with spending of $8,327 and $7,474 per student compared to the national average of $11,934. Also, like teacher salary issues, not only were these state expenditures relatively low as compared to other states, but they were also low compared to prior spending levels. In 2015, 29 states had lower state per-pupil funding than they did in 2008, including Arizona, North Carolina, Oklahoma, and Kentucky (Leachman et al., 2017). Between 2008 and 2017, Arizona's state education funding had been reduced by 14%. During that same time, Oklahoma's funding for education was reduced by 28%, leading to larger class sizes, a lack of supplies and learning materials, outdated textbooks, elimination of extracurricular activities, crumbling infrastructure, inadequate learning equipment, and a 4-day school week for many schools across the state (Blanc, 2019).

Both these targets of teacher strikes—low teacher compensation and underinvestment in education—are direct policy outcomes of the A

Nation at Risk paradigm. This paradigm, and particularly the ways in which it is informed by neoliberalism, has led to severe cuts to education spending as government is starved of revenue and education funds are diverted to private entities. Under the market logics of neoliberalism, private entities governed by the free market are prioritized over public goods. Government is seen as inefficient and failing to meet market demands. This leads to a disinvestment in public services as funds are shifted to private entities to provide those services. Additionally, because government is seen as inefficient, neoliberalism's market logic also leads to a reduction in total government revenue, through tax cuts and other financial benefits given to corporations.

Ironically, the *A Nation at Risk* report itself called for greater teacher salaries and educational spending, but the paradigm that has been informed by it has resulted in profound disinvestment in public education. For example, in Arizona, which is often dominated by conservative politics in which neoliberal ideologies have established a strong ideological foothold, the state legislature had cut taxes every year but one since 1990, which is one reason state expenditures on education declined by 14% from 2008 to 2017 (Turner et al., 2018). Oklahoma, another deeply conservative state, had not raised taxes since 1990 and, like Arizona, had actually cut taxes since 2008, leading to nearly a billion dollars in lost revenue for the state, accounting in part for its 28% reduction in state spending on education since 2008 (Blanc, 2019). In fact, of the six states to experience widespread teacher strikes, five had lower state education spending in 2018 than they did in 2008, and three of those had recently cut taxes despite increased state revenues since 2008 (Leachman et al., 2017).

The A Nation at Risk paradigm has also contributed to lower teacher compensation through the overall reduction in education spending, the de-professionalization of teachers, and the weakening of teachers' unions. While teachers may have been undercompensated throughout American history, with less money being spent on education under the paradigm, there is less money for teachers' salaries and compensation, like retirement benefits and health care. Compounding this is the paradigm's sustained de-professionalization of the teaching profession. Coupled with the paradigm's narrative of teachers and school leaders bearing the responsibility for America's failing schools, this positioning of teachers justifies low teacher compensation and provides ideological support for policymakers who seek to divert public spending to private entities and limit the political power of public employees. Indeed, the A Nation at Risk paradigm has been particularly antagonistic toward teachers' unions, who are often seen as antithetical to its policy prescriptions, which both justifies and facilitates low teacher compensation. Thus, the teacher strikes of 2018, in responding to low teacher compensation and reductions in education spending, were directly rejecting the policy outcomes of the A Nation at Risk paradigm.

Students, too, were responding to a constellation of circumstances and policies that grew out of the A Nation at Risk paradigm and the ideologies that inform it. The individual right to bear arms holds a privileged position within the collection of ideologies that animate the paradigm. Neoconservatism and authoritarian populism, with their focus on individuals, individual rights, and a general distrust of government, have made gun rights a staple of modern conservative politics. In support of this right, the National Rifle Association (NRA) has spent over $200 million between 1998 and 2016 on political activities in support of gun rights, in opposition to gun control legislation, and in support of sympathetic, predominately Republican, politicians (Jacobson, 2017). Further solidifying the place of the individual right to bear arms in modern conservativism, the Supreme Court held for the first time in America's history in 2008 that the Second Amendment to the U.S. Constitution protects an individual's right to bear arms (*District of Columbia v. Heller*, 2008) and that this right was enforceable against the states as well as the federal government (*McDonald v. Chicago*, 2010). These policies and ideologies have facilitated the proliferation of guns in America, with Americans owning an estimated 390 million guns, or approximately 120 firearms per 100 residents (BBC News, 2019).

Corresponding with the proliferation of guns in American society, school shootings have become a recurring incident in America's schools. While schools remain empirically one of the safest spaces for students, between the Columbine shooting in 1999, in which 13 people were killed and another 21 injured, and 2019 there were 238 shootings at primary and secondary schools immediately before, during, or shortly after the school day (Cox et al., 2019). These shootings have directly impacted over 228,000 students who have experienced gun violence at their schools. Indirectly, though, the proliferation of school shootings has led school administrators and policymakers to enact policies and procedures to prevent and respond to the threat of school shooters, leading students since the Columbine shooting to grow up in what Cameron Kasky, a cofounder of March for Our Lives, calls the "the school shooting generation" (Kasky, 2018, p. 7). Students who have grown up in schools since Columbine have been subjected to active shooter drills, increased surveillance, the presence of school resource officers, and tighter regulation and control.

These policies have grown out of the ideologies of the A Nation at Risk paradigm and have mirrored and exacerbated the crime control paradigm that has dominated school discipline since 1983. The accountability regime fostered by the paradigm requires greater and greater means of coercion from schools to achieve student compliance with the paradigm's policy prescriptions. Thus, as schools become more accountable for students' standardized test scores and narrow the curriculum toward preparing students for these tests, schools require additional mechanisms to compel students to engage with this new curriculum. This has led to tighter regulation and control of students in schools through greater punishments, increased surveillance of students, and the increased presence of school resource officers on campus, all of which have contributed to making schools policed spaces. Within this perspective, the threat of school violence requires a militant response, explaining such activities as active shooter drills for students, the proposed arming of teachers, and an erosion of students' privacy rights.

The students of Parkland and across the country who protested in the spring of 2018 were protesting both to prevent another tragedy like the one at Marjory Stoneman Douglas (MSD) High School and to challenge the ways in which being part of the school shooting generation had impacted their experiences in school. In describing what led students of MSD to organize the March for Our Lives, David Hogg (MSD class of 2018) wrote:

> But we're all really different people. We don't even have the same opinions on gun control. The only thing we share completely is what Lauren [Hogg] said when she was getting started—we were all born after Columbine, we all grew up with Sandy Hook and terrorism and code-red active-shooter drills. We all have grown up conditioned to be afraid. *And we're all sick and tired of being afraid.* (Hogg & Hogg, 2018, p. 19, emphasis in original)

Here, David Hogg positions the activism of the March for Our Lives organizers as being in response to both the tragedy at MSD and the impacts that school shootings have had on their educational experiences. They were responding not only to the shooting itself but also to the ways in which the threat of school shootings has shaped their experiences in schools. The student protesters were responding to how they had been conditioned to be fearful at school due to both the frequency of school shootings and the policies that schools implement to prevent and respond to them.

The student protestors of 2018 had come to see schools as dangerous places and, at the same time, had become numb to the reality of school shootings. Cameron Kasky (MSD class of 2019) wrote of his reaction immediately after the Parkland shooting:

> It wasn't until I sat down in my father's car, knowing that my brother and at least most of my close friends—the ones who hadn't lost their phones and were able to text—were alive, that the thought came upon me: this whole time, I had been way too comfortable. Now, my reality was becoming clear. I knew that I was part of a flavor-of-the-month mass school shooting. The fact that I could easily identify this phenomenon speaks volumes for just how common this is and just how desensitized we have been to these horrific acts. (Kasky, 2018, p. 7)

Similarly, David Hogg, who interviewed a classmate while hiding at school during the Parkland shooting, recounted how the classmate had texted her two sisters that there was as a shooting at her school but that she was fine, and how her sisters had both responded with "OMG, LOL, you're funny" (Hogg & Hogg, 2018, p. 96). The students who organized the March for Our Lives, like student protesters across the country, were protesting because they could no longer tolerate the ways in which school shootings had become an expected and, at least seemingly by the larger society, tolerated part of their lives. In this way, these students—like their teachers— were responding directly to the policy outcomes of the A Nation at Risk paradigm.

The outcomes of these student protests and teacher strikes also demonstrate how these activities constituted direct attacks on the policy outcomes of the A Nation at Risk paradigm. While the impacts of these protests and strikes were mixed and are still reverberating through our political landscape, the student and teacher civic activists of 2018 had profound impacts on educational policy. For the statewide teacher strikes, the strikes in West Virginia, Oklahoma, and Arizona resulted in increased salaries for teachers and school support staff. Similarly, the strikes in Oklahoma, Kentucky, and Colorado led to greater funding for education in those states (Yan, 2018). Although none of these teacher strikes achieved all their policy goals, each strike succeeded in some way to reverse the policy outcomes of the paradigm's systemic disinvestment of education. For the 2018 student protests, aimed as they were at national issues that find expression in local schools and communities, the results of these protests were more diffuse. These students brought significant societal attention to the issue of gun violence in schools and the ways in which it shapes students' experiences. In the year after the Parkland shooting, state legislatures passed 67 gun control or gun violence prevention bills into law. In addition, the 2018 student protests influenced the national dialogue on guns and led to more young people participating in politics. Following the 2018 student protests, many of which focused on increasing youth political participation, the 2018 November midterm elections saw youth voter turnout increase from 21% to 31%, the highest youth turnout rate in decades (Beckett, 2019). Thus, like the statewide teachers' strikes, the student protests of 2018 also led to results that are inimical to the A Nation at Risk paradigm, including the ways in which it positions both students and teachers within educational policy.

Students and Teachers' 2018 Civic Activism as a Rejection of How the A Nation at Risk Paradigm Positions Them Within Educational Policy

Even as the student and teacher activists of the spring of 2018 challenged the policy outcomes of the A Nation at Risk paradigm, their activities were made possible by their rebellion against the ways in which they are positioned and understood within that paradigm. The teachers were rejecting the ways in which this paradigm positions them as passive policy martyrs who are required to passively acquiesce to educational policy decisions that ask them to do more, with and for less, and with less voice. The students were also rejecting political passivity as they challenged dominant narratives about school shootings and about the proper place of young people in politics. Understood in this way, the student protests and teacher strikes constitute both a rejection of the outcomes of the A Nation at Risk paradigm as well as its reframing of their citizenship and civic agency.

Matt Bevin, Kentucky's governor during the state's protests, perfectly captured the ways in which this paradigm positions teachers. After teacher strikes closed schools throughout the state and teachers demonstrated at the state capitol, in a statement to reporters, Governor Bevin said, "I guarantee you somewhere in Kentucky today, a child was sexually assaulted that was left at home because there was nobody there to watch them." He continued, "Children were harmed—some physically, some sexually, some were introduced to drugs for the first time—because they were vulnerable and left alone" (Horton, 2018). Although Bevin later apologized for his statement, his remarks in response to the statewide teacher activism that was rocking Kentucky are indicative of the A Nation at Risk paradigm's view of teachers as passive policy martyrs. By alleging that students were harmed due to the teacher walkouts—despite having no factual basis for his remarks—Bevin positioned teachers as being responsible for students' safety and well-being, even when those students are not at school. Bevin's statements insinuated that teachers were being selfish by striking. They were overstepping the expectations of their profession, and in doing so they were jeopardizing the well-being of their students. Given the context of these comments, delivered while teachers were protesting for greater funding for education and greater financial compensation for teachers, Bevin's remarks imply that teachers should forgo advocating for these things for the sake of their students. Instead, he implies that teachers should passively accept the outcomes of the A Nation at Risk paradigm, including the low pay and lack of professionalism that negatively impact them, sacrificing themselves for their students. The teachers engaged in the 2018 teacher strikes explicitly rejected this positioning of teachers.

Prior to going on strike, one West Virginia teacher exclaimed in a social media post that the teacher's strike was necessary because "we are human beings" (Blanc, 2019, p. 24). This teacher was calling for greater respect for teachers and the teaching profession and positioned the strike as necessary to break a cycle of teacher de-professionalization and victimization, both of which are results of the A Nation at Risk paradigm (Bocking, 2018). The 2018 teacher strikes challenged this positioning and the ways in which teachers are asked to do more and are held more tightly accountable, while having less autonomy and receiving less compensation. As part of the A Nation at Risk paradigm's disinvestment in education, teachers are less well compensated in many states and have fewer resources for education. Additionally, fewer teachers are available for more students. Since 2009, there are approximately 1.5 million more students in America but 135,000 fewer public school employees (Blanc, 2019). Perfectly capturing teachers' rejection of this state of affairs, one West Virginia teacher in a letter to her students explained why she was protesting: "I love you and that's why I'm doing this" (Blanc, 2019, p. 79).

In engaging in these strikes, teachers were also rejecting their position within the A Nation at Risk paradigm as passive recipients of policy decisions made by elites who are more centralized and less local. This shift in who makes educational policy, coupled with sustained attacks on teacher unions, has limited teachers' ability to influence policy. At the same time, teachers are positioned within educational policy as compliance operatives who merely implement the policy decisions of others. Viewed from within this paradigm, the only choices available to teachers are for them to accept the status quo or leave teaching. Dunn (2018), in a study of published teacher resignation letters, argues that the teachers who write these letters are seeking to reclaim their agency within the A Nation at Risk paradigm by resigning and publicly speaking back to the political forces that they see as causing the circumstances that led them to resign. Taken together, this explains why, in a recent Gallup poll, only 31% of teachers said that teachers have a great deal of influence over educational policy, but 97% said that teachers should have such influence (Hodges, 2018). The 2018 teacher strikes responded to this disconnect, even in the face of sustained political resistance.

In all the states that experienced teacher strikes, public sector strikes are prohibited by law (Blanc, 2019). Additionally, many of these states had weak public unions due to restrictions on collective bargaining and "right to work" laws. In Arizona, prior to the statewide strike, only 25% of teachers belonged to a union or professional organization. In Oklahoma, this number was 40% (Blanc, 2019). This meant that the teachers who were engaged in these strikes did so despite the threat of legal retaliation by state leaders. In West Virginia, the attorney general warned teachers prior to the strike:

> A work stoppage of any length on any ground is illegal. Let us make no mistake, the impending work stoppage is unlawful. State law and court rulings give specific parties avenues to remedy such illegal conduct, including the option to seek an injunction to end an unlawful strike. (Blanc, 2019, p. 50)

Similarly, in Arizona, the state superintendent repeatedly threatened teachers with the loss of their jobs if they walked out. Under the laws of each of these states, it would have been completely lawful to terminate, suspend, or fine every teacher who engaged in these strikes, a tool that state leaders attempted to use to dissuade any potential collective action by teachers.

Yet, despite these threats, which can be read within the A Nation at Risk paradigm as attempts to enforce teachers' position within educational policy as passive policy martyrs, these teachers struck and, in doing so, realized their collective civic agency. As one Arizona educator reflected, "During the walkout I felt more empowered and respected as a teacher than ever before. We all get that 'I'm so sorry' look when we say we are teachers. I never experienced that once. I was suddenly an activist and hero" (Blanc, 2019, p. 87). Noah Karvelis, a #RedForEd organizer, said of the protests that "educators saw that they have power. They've realized that they're exploited and that they have structural power. And in this walkout, they made their power felt" (Blanc, 2019, p. 97). These teachers became political through participating in collective action. It was through exercising their civic agency that they realized their agency and rejected passive conceptions of citizenship that had been foisted on them by the A Nation at Risk paradigm. Indeed, these protests led to spikes in union membership in these states as, for example, over 2,000 teachers in West Virginia and 2,500 teachers in Arizona joined one of their state's teacher unions (Blanc, 2019). In the words of one Arizona educator: "The word 'union' does not scare me anymore. I joined the Arizona Education Association and plan on continuing to fight for what is right for education and students. I feel the most empowered I have ever felt as an educator and now do believe that change is possible" (Blanc, 2019, p. 8).

Like their teachers, student protesters were also rejecting the ways in which the A Nation at Risk paradigm positions them as passive consumers of education policy. Within this paradigm, students are simultaneously viewed as the products of education, the consumers of education, and—at least for some students—threats to education. However, by staging walkouts, marching, and engaging in political lobbying, these students were not silently accepting the status quo; they were actively participating in creating a new one. In order to reject the paradigm's view of them as passive consumers of education, these students had to overcome two entrenched beliefs about primary and secondary students and their place within education policy. First, they had to grapple with the established narrative of school shootings and gun violence in schools, which portrays students as tragic, but silent, victims of gun violence. Second, they had to confront and overcome perceptions based on their age that they were not legitimate participants in political discourse. Overcoming these assumptions made these students' protests especially meaningful within a paradigm that actively discourages student civic agency.

Cameron Kasky (MSD class of 2019), in recounting his thoughts immediately after the shooting and his motivation for cofounding the March for Our Lives organization, wrote:

The rules are set up for Marjory Stoneman Douglas to become a part of the American School Shooting Machine. I remembered the usual narrative: Small town. Good, humble people. Some lone wolf shoots up the school. He is a misunderstood, socially ostracized kid. It was a mental health thing. Somehow, mental health shot up a school. . . . The people of our country, while deeply hurt and truly affected, will eat it up. Flowers will be sent, cards will be written to the students ("Sorry your school got shot up!"), and thoughts and prayers will be tossed around like a common cold at a state college. Then the flowers will wilt, the people in the school and in the town will try to begin to heal, and somewhere, another school will be shot up. . . . It happens so often that the entire cycle has become routine. (Kasky, 2018, pp. 3–4)

After the Parkland shooting, Kasky was motivated to change the narrative of school shootings and the role that the students who experience them play in these narratives. Within the traditional narrative, the students who experience school shootings are seen as sympathetic victims of an inevitable but isolated incident caused by a single bad actor. They passively receive the well wishes of a captive audience, who then quickly moves on to the next tragedy. In his remarks, Kasky indicates that one of his goals in engaging in the work of the March for Our Lives organization was to reclaim the narrative of the Parkland shooting for the students who experienced it: "This is not the media's narrative. This is not their story. This is nobody's tragedy to interpret but our own" (Kasky, 2018, p. 5). In doing so, he—like hundreds of thousands of students across the country—rejected the passive role that the A Nation at Risk paradigm had cast him in and established that students have an important perspective that ought to be heard within educational policy.

However, being heard and being accepted were very different things to the students who protested following the Parkland shooting. These students had to grapple not only with how they were understood within the narrative of school shootings but also how society views young adults and their political participation. A host of the popular *Fox & Friends Weekend* show perfectly captured this challenge when he remarked in response to the activism of March for Our Lives, "Spare me if I don't want to hear the sanctimoniousness of a seventeen-year-old" (Hogg & Hogg, 2018, p. 120). As this statement demonstrates, the student activists of the 2018 protests were often seen as illegitimate participants in political dialogue; it just wasn't the accepted place of students to engage in political discourse.

For these students, though, their age was often an asset that allowed them to challenge this idea and to ultimately speak out and have their voices heard. Being young and already being labeled outsiders within political discourse allowed these students to engage politically in ways that defied established norms and decorum. In a memorable exchange with Senator Marco Rubio during a CNN townhall, Kasky repeatedly asked Senator Rubio if he would refuse to accept campaign funds from the NRA, even interrupting the senator when he attempted to shift the conversation. Kasky later remarked on the Bill Maher show, "We don't respect you just because you have a 'senator' in front of your name" (Hogg & Hogg, 2018, p. 113). As

David Hogg (MSD class of 2018) observed, the students of the March for Our Lives movement weren't going to play the game of normal decorum because, as political outsiders, they didn't have to. For these students, "Respect wouldn't have goaded Rubio into baring his teeth on Twitter. And decorum wouldn't have gotten us on the Bill Maher show or CNN or MSNBC or all the other shows that wanted us to tell the story again and again. People really like the kid who finally says the emperor is naked" (Hogg & Hogg, 2018, p. 116). These students flipped the script on their age, turning it into a political asset as they challenged assumptions about the place of young adults in political discourse.

Ultimately, through their activism, these students challenged how society views students within the school shooting generation and how it views the political participation of young people. In doing so, they—like the teachers who rejected their positioning as passive policy martyrs—rejected the way in which the A Nation at Risk paradigm positions them as passive consumers and products of educational policy.

Latent and Burgeoning Resistance to the A Nation at Risk Paradigm: Shadow Spaces and a Realignment of the Educational Policy Landscape as Incubators of Student and Teacher Civic Agency

In addition to responding to the policy outcomes of the A Nation at Risk paradigm and the ways in which it positions students and teachers in educational policy, the 2018 student and teacher civic activism also coalesced around shadow spaces created by the paradigm. These shadow spaces—understood as spaces that exist largely outside the influences of dominant political, cultural, or societal values and beliefs in which individuals and communities can explore and promote nondominant values and ideas—existed outside the A Nation at Risk paradigm. Social media was perhaps the most significant shadow space for both students and teachers. It allowed teachers to organize outside of existing political structures and to create broad advocacy coalitions, which themselves served as liminal shadow spaces for teacher activism. Likewise, students used social media and the internet to gain recognition, popularize their messages, and organize massive nationwide networks of protest. Another important shadow space for students, especially the Parkland students who organized the March for Our Lives, were their schools and teachers, who embraced a curriculum and pedagogy that promoted knowledge, skills, and dispositions that fell outside of those privileged by the A Nation at Risk paradigm. Engaging in these shadow spaces allowed these students and teachers to create their civic movements, growing as they did to realign the politics of education to advance interests that had not been represented within larger political structures.

Through social media sites like Facebook, Instagram, and Twitter, the student and teachers of 2018 were able to create massive state and national movements. These social media platforms gave these students and teachers a forum through which to amplify their voices, have their voices heard without being mediated through others, and organize with like-minded people to advocate for societal change (Thapliyal, 2018). Many of the teacher strikes found their genesis in Facebook groups that existed outside of existing teacher unions. These groups included West Virginia Pubic Employees United, Oklahoma Teachers United, Oklahoma Teacher Walkout-The Time is Now!, and Arizona Educators United. As one West Virginia teacher said of the West Virginia group, "The United group became like one big faculty room where we could connect with other teachers and workers throughout the state" (Blanc, 2019, p. 61). These teachers used these groups to discuss and solidify the goals, methods, and strategies of pushing for systemic change.

These social media groups also allowed these teachers to overcome geographic and political boundaries between schools, districts, unions, and teachers. For example, in West Virginia there were three different teacher unions, and overcoming the political in-fighting and geographic isolation of school districts was one of the primary motivators for creating the state's Facebook group. This allowed the participation of all 55 of the state's school districts in the teacher strike (Blanc, 2019). Likewise, in Arizona, the Arizona Educators United group allowed the growing teacher movement there to cultivate a network of 2,000 school-based volunteer organizer-representatives, most of whom had no prior organizing or activist experiences. Through these organizer-representatives, the group—which started on March 5, 2018—was able to mobilize massive grassroots support among teachers to push for a statewide strike. Beginning in mid-April, the group began asking its supporters to wear red and started to stage "walk-ins" of teachers at their schools to continue building solidarity and support. These activities culminated in the April 26th statewide strike that affected over 1,000 schools across the state. For the teachers of the 2018 strikes, social media was a powerful tool because it allowed them to cultivate broad networks of support outside of existing political structures, free from the constraints and entrenched institutional positions of those groups.

Students also relied on social media as an important shadow space in which to grow and promote their movement. Indeed, one of the primary student protests, the National School Walkout, was created as a Change.org petition by 16-year-old high school sophomore Lane Murdock. There was no national organization that planned and promoted this protest. Instead, it was proposed by Murdock and promoted by students through social media, who then created their own local chapters and plans. Only after the protest gained momentum on social media did Murdock and others create the National School Walkout organization to help coordinate protests and offer them resources (Gray, 2018).

In addition to using social media to organize protests across the country in timeframes that would have been unthinkable to students in the 1960s and '70s, students used social media to advocate and challenge entrenched political opposition to their agenda. As David Hogg (MSD class of 2018) put it:

> [Social media] is just the way our generation has communicated our entire lives, and it turned out to be the perfect way to deal with [critics of the March for Our Lives movement]—you may have the Second Amendment and guns, Wayne LaPierre, but we have the First Amendment and Twitter. (Hogg & Hogg, 2018, p. 120)

Echoing this point, John Barnitt (MSD class of 2019), Sarah Chadwick (MSD class of 2019), and Sofie Whitney (MSD class of 2018), who were also cocreators of the March for Our Lives organization, wrote:

> Social media has given us the platform to say what we want to say and reach millions of people. We took advantage of that, and it kept us in people's minds because they were hearing from us directly: not the news stations, just direct information that we were putting out ourselves. . . . We didn't need the approval of anyone to speak our minds. We were unfiltered and unapologetic. The power for real change was in our back pockets this whole time, we just didn't realize it. (Barnitt et al., 2018, p. 42)

Indeed, the social media use of the March for Our Lives organizers is an important reason their movement gained such a wide following. The story of March for Our Lives is replete with viral Twitter posts and hashtags that worked to change the script on school shootings and allowed the students to create their movement.

One of the first things the Parkland students who launched March for Our Lives did upon creating their movement was come up with and popularize the Twitter hashtag #NeverAgain. Within a few hours of using this hashtag, which allows Twitter users to search for similar messages and also allows Twitter to publicize hashtags that are being widely used, #NeverAgain was one of the most used hashtags on Twitter. According to the March for Our Lives organizers, this moment was when the students of March for Our Lives realized that they could have a real impact:

> After a couple of hours, and a couple hundred tweets featuring that hashtag, #NeverAgain trended at number two, right under Drake's "God's Plan." I think that might have been the moment we realized the impact that our voices could have. If we could take over the internet, even briefly, with just a two-word hashtag, the distance to which our words could stretch could be infinite. We always had a voice, but now we had an audience. (Barnitt et al., 2018, p. 45)

Within days of the Parkland shooting and the popularization of #NeverAgain, the students of the March for Our Lives organization had thousands of Twitter followers and their tweets were reaching a wide audience. This allowed them to immediately and, often cleverly, respond to opposition and actively promote their message directly to their audience. Here are just a few notable examples that gained national recognition and helped propel the students' movement:

- Lauren Hogg (MSD class of 2021) who, responding to Donald Trump Jr.'s promotion of conspiracy theories about David Hogg and the Parkland shooting, tweeted "Hey @FLOTUS [First Lady Melania Trump] you say that your mission as First Lady is to stop cyber bullying, well then, don't you think it would have been smart to have a convo with your step-son @DonaldJTrumpJr before he liked a post about a false conspiracy theory which in turn put a target on my back" (Hogg & Hogg, 2018, p. 82).
- Delaney Tarr (MSD class of 2018) who called out politicians for accepted NRA funding with the tweet, "To every lawmaker out there: No longer can you take money from the @NRA. No longer can you fly under the radar doing whatever it is that you want to do" (Hogg & Hogg, 2018, p. 108).
- Sarah Chadwick (MSD class of 2019) who quipped in a tweet, "We should change the name of AR-15s to 'Marco Rubio' because they are so easy to buy." This led to students wearing $1.05 signs at protests across Florida to symbolize the amount of money per Florida student that Senator Rubio had received in campaign contributions from the NRA (Hogg & Hogg, 2018, pp. 114–115).

Through their use of social media, which for these students existed as a shadow space outside of dominant political control, the students who organized the March for Our Lives and students across the country were able to promote their messages, recapture a national dialogue, and organize their national protest movement.

Another important shadow space for the student protestors were schools and teachers that operated outside of the A Nation at Risk paradigm to prepare and support students in their exercise of civic agency. This paradigm has led to schools narrowing the curriculum, neglecting and neutering civic education, and prioritizing the knowledge and skills necessary for economic participation. Despite these influences, throughout the country, pockets of resistance exist in which the hold of the paradigm is not ubiquitous. These spaces are often created by teachers and school leaders who hold beliefs about teaching and learning that run counter to this paradigm and who have not experienced the full effects of its emphasis on accountability. These effects are typically felt most fiercely at schools with low academic achievement as measured by standardized tests, which is highly correlated to the socioeconomic status of the school and its students (Darling-Hammond,

2010). It was within these spaces that the student activists learned to exercise their civic agency, as teachers and school leaders, who were often more closely aligned with democratic and community-oriented ideals about education, supported them in doing so.

For the students of March for Our Lives, many of them recognize their experiences at MSD as empowering them to create their nationwide movement: "Stoneman Douglas is a big piece, too, because the teachers there put such a huge emphasis on studying real problems in the world today, so we already knew a lot about politics and social issues and just presumed that we could do something about them" (Hogg & Hogg, 2018, p. 21). MSD is located in Parkland, Florida, an affluent suburb of Fort Lauderdale. In the 2018–2019 school year, while the school's per-pupil expenditures were lower than the Florida state average ($7,776 as compared to $8,560), less than 20% of the school's students qualified as economically disadvantaged (Florida Department of Education, n.d.). MSD also boasts strong academics, receiving an "A" in 2018–2019 on its state report card. For the 2018–2019 school year, MSD beat the state average for students scoring proficient or better on statewide assessments by 17.4% for English language arts (74.3% to 56.9%), 6.7% for mathematics (66.3% to 59.6%), 24.7% for science (82.5% to 57.8%), and 8.4% for social studies (80.6% to 72.2%). It was within this context that MSD and its teachers were able to offer a curriculum and provide spaces to help students develop their civic agency, even in the face of the A Nation at Risk paradigm.

At MSD, many of the March for Our Lives students had taken classes such as TV production, debate, civics, journalism, and drama. These classes helped prepare the Parkland students to achieve what they did in the face of their shared tragedy. According to Melissa Falkowski, the MSD journalism teacher:

> The strength of Marjory Stoneman Douglas High School's journalism programs prepared our student journalists to be at the forefront of the rallying cry of #NeverAgain after the devastating tragedy at our school on February 14, 2018. These students were already adept at using their voices to call for change within their school and community. They used their training to speak out on TV, on social media, and in articles published nationally and globally. The nation has been impressed with the strength, poise, rational thinking, and compelling arguments. Many of these students were part of one of the school's various media programs—the newspaper, TV production, the yearbook, or the literary magazine. (Falkowski, 2018, p. 13)

Similarly, Eric Garner, the MSD broadcasting teacher, recounts how "most of the key players you have seen in the media were, or are, in my television production class. The 'crisis actors' trained here daily. . . . My class was part of the activists' training" (Garner, 2018, p. 17).

These accounts were echoed by many MSD students who credited their classes as preparing them for their activism and who recognized their teachers as role models of civic engagement. Rebecca Schneid (MSD class of 2019) captured both these ideas when she wrote:

> From the beginning, Mrs. Falkowski set an amazing example for us. She started speaking out on the day of the shooting, just as angry as the rest of us that this was able to happen at our school. She took the lead, making sure we understood our role and responsibility as the reporters for our school newspaper. She pushed us toward excellence when writing and designing our memorial issue, our activism special issue called "Taking a Stand," and our online stories. Without her fierce leadership, we would never have had the courage to use our newspaper and our reporting to educate and influence others. (Schneid, 2018, pp. 32–33)

The students of Parkland, when faced with tragedy and a platform to speak on it, fell back on their experiences in classes like journalism and TV production. Delaney Tarr (MSD class of 2018) talked about how "a level of instinct kicked in among some of us" when confronted with cameras and interviews based on their experiences in school as "journalists, drama performers, debaters, and student government representatives" (Tarr, 2018, p. 59). According to David Hogg (MSD class of 2018) these classes taught the March for Our Lives organizers "basically everything we needed to understand to keep our movement from fading out" (Hogg & Hogg, 2018, p. 46).

Even as the shadow spaces of social media and empowering schools, teachers, and colleagues offered the student and teacher activists spaces to grow and develop their activism, each of these movements grew in ways that challenge how the A Nation at Risk paradigm structures educational policy. Teacher-activists directed their collective agency at state lawmakers rather than local school districts. Similarly, students injected their voices and perspectives into national debates over guns and gun violence; policy debates that had previously lacked this perspective even as students were deeply impacted by their outcomes. These strategic decisions echo the "venue shopping" that occurs when interest groups shift the political battleground from a typically hostile or ossified political forum to another (Baumgartner & Jones, 1993; Pralle, 2003). In venue shopping, groups seek venues that are more receptive to the group's interests or its framing of a particular policy problem. Even if the new venue is not more receptive, it must at a minimum renavigate the policy conflict from within a different institutional context that has its own considerations, interest groups, and limitations. Typically, new forums involve both existing policy actors as well as new interest groups that are unique to the forum or that have greater access to it. By viewing these students' and teachers' activities as restructuring the political landscape of educational policy under the A Nation at Risk paradigm rather than as engaging in strategic venue shopping, however, we are better able to understand how paradigms influence and structure politics (Mehta, 2013) and how those politics in turn structure how groups access and participate in and across various policy venues.

Since the 1970s, teacher unions have largely focused their attention on legal recognition and protections for their members. Often, this has meant that teacher unions have directed their activities at the district level to engage in collective bargaining on behalf of the district's teachers. However, this has limited both the scope of the issues that teacher unions can address and their geographic power. Collective bargaining focuses primarily on the working conditions and compensation of teachers, and because it happens at the district level, it often pits teachers against communities and impedes the ability of teacher unions to realize statewide or systemic change. For the states that experienced statewide teacher protests, the teacher advocacy groups who planned and coordinated these protests stepped outside of this framework.

West Virginia, the fuse that sparked the 2018 teacher strike movement, is a perfect example of this. West Virginia has a strong culture of public unions with over 70% of its teachers belonging to unions. However, this membership is split among three different unions, the American Federation of Teachers-West Virginia (AFT-WV), the West Virginia Education Association (WVEA), and the West Virginia School Service Personnel Association (WVSSPA), who all compete for membership. Prior to the statewide teacher protests, these unions focused primarily on engaging in collective bargaining with local districts, which is permissible in West Virginia but not mandated. In order to create statewide pressure about teacher salaries, West Virginian teachers created the West Virginia Public Employees United (WVPEU) Facebook group. Through this group, these teachers organized teachers in all 55 of the state's districts to support a teacher strike for greater pay. It was only after months of pressure from members of the WVPEU and their own members that the three West Virginian teacher unions began collaborating with the WVPEU in support of the strike, which began on February 22. However, the strike went "wildcat" on February 28 after the presidents of the WVEU and the AFT-WV announced to the crowd of teachers and school employees gathered at the statehouse that a deal had been struck and that the strike was over. Instead of ending the strike after the union presidents had called for it to end, West Virginia's teachers continued to strike. The union presidents' announcement was met with chants of "55 united," "Fix it now," "Back to the table," and "We are the union bosses." The strike would continue until March 7, when the governor signed a 5% pay increase for teachers and school staff (Blanc, 2019).

As the trajectory of the West Virginia teachers' strike demonstrates, the relationships between teacher social media advocacy groups and their teacher unions were often complex. West Virginia's teachers created a state-wide organization to put pressure on their state legislature because their unions were reluctant and ill-positioned to do so. They then denied their union leadership and continued to strike even after the union presidents called for the strike to end. Teacher advocacy groups in other states likewise initiated their states' protests, putting pressure on teacher unions to align themselves with their movements. In Arizona and Oklahoma, teacher advocacy groups also initiated the pressure for the statewide teacher strikes, and it was only later that the states' unions joined and contributed to their efforts.

These teacher advocacy groups grew into political spaces that had been left open by traditional teacher unions and the ways that the A Nation at Risk paradigm structures the politics of educational policy. Unlike existing teacher unions, these advocacy groups coalesced around broad, systemic goals and aimed their advocacy at state policymakers rather than at local districts. Importantly, these advocacy groups often positioned themselves as intentionally separate from partisan politics and avoided politically charged issues such as racism and racial inequalities in schools. Representatives of the advocacy groups in each of the states estimated that their membership consisted of approximately 45% Democrats, 40% Republicans, and 15% independents (Blanc, 2019). This broad ideological support was made possible through these advocacy groups' focus on broad policy goals and their avoidance of partisan politics, which in many ways had limited the effectiveness of teacher unions in their states. Also enabling the broad support of these advocacy groups was their approach to cultivating collective support and being inclusive of all school personnel. These advocacy groups built their movements from the ground up through dialogue—often through their social media pages—and collaboration. The goals and activities of these groups grew out of these collaborative conversations rather than being handed down through a hierarchical structure. Crucial to the success of these groups, they also included school personnel like custodians, cooks, bus drivers, teachers' aids, and substitute teachers within their movement and within their policy goals. In West Virginia particularly, this coalition proved to be crucial because bus drivers and other school support staff were among the first to reject the proposed compromise offered by union leaders on February 27, leading the strike to become wildcat as schools were forced to remain closed.

Together, the way these groups positioned themselves to reorganize the politics of education allowed these groups to build broad coalitions of support that included school support staff as well as students, parents, and community members. Rather than pitting teachers against communities, these groups were able to cultivate broad community support through outreach campaigns and direct lobbying of parents and communities. Teachers throughout these strikes repeated the mantra that "teacher working conditions are students' learning conditions." Through their collaborative approach—which allowed them to expand their policy aims to include both increased compensation for teachers and greater funding for education—these teachers were able to fill a void left by traditional teacher unions and achieve unprecedented concessions from state lawmakers.

The student movement of 2018 also worked to reorganize the politics of education under the A Nation at Risk paradigm by disrupting partisan deadlock on issues of gun control that had neglected the perspectives of young people who are directly impacted by these policies. In one of the first and most impassioned public statements by a Parkland student, David Hogg (MSD class of 2018), on the night of the shooting, pleaded with the public, "We're the kids, you're the grown-ups. Please do something" (Hogg & Hogg, 2018, p. 18). In many ways, the 2018 student movement came about because David's plea went—and had gone—unanswered. Instead, the students themselves had to step in to advocate for change. These students were responding to a cycle of tragedy that both ignored their perspective and that had grown to be dominated by entrenched and intransigent political forces. As the students of March for Our Lives put it:

> Tragedies like the one at our high school have been a consistent reflection of America's greatest flaws in the twenty-first century, but substantial action has not been taken by those in power, and the people of this country are confused and angry. The root of this frustrating cycle has long been a problem in America: our politicians' interest in being reelected and paid overshadows their interest in the common good of the people. This betrayal has been particularly prevalent with school shootings. (Barnitt et al., 2018, p. 40)

These students explicitly understood their advocacy as filling a void in public discourse based on collective action rather than special interest. Unlike their teachers—who reorganized and redirected an existing political bloc—the student protesters emerged as new political participants with a unique perspective that brought new pressure to an ossified political impasse.

While these student movements were mobilizing a new generation of political participants, they did so in ways very similar to those of their teachers. The student protests were largely generated from grassroots organizations, with little central coordination and with broad policy goals developed through collaboration and dialogue. Of the nationally organized student protests, the #ENOUGH National School Walkout planned by the Women's March was the only protest planned by an existing advocacy group, and even then, the organization of each march throughout the country was left to students at local schools. This was also true for the March for Our Lives and the National School Walkout, both of which were implemented by local students and community leaders who took responsibility for organizing their local activities. The students of March for Our Lives in particular embraced this fragmented and democratic structure as they grew their movement through collaboration and individual efforts:

> People ask us how we came up with our "publicity campaigns." The answer is, we didn't. We're really disorganized. Plus we're teenagers, so none of us likes to be told what to do. But that turned out to be the best idea we didn't have, because it takes a lot of individual thought and individual initiative to be that disorganized. Nobody asked for permission or approval—if they thought of something that seemed like it could work, they just did it. Some people did a lot of interviews; some people were really good at Twitter; other people focused on organizing and coordinating. (Hogg & Hogg, 2018, p. 103)

It was through these grassroots, disorganized but coordinated efforts that the student protests of 2018 were able to grow and challenge the impasse on gun regulation in American politics. These students were adding a new voice—one that had been excluded from contemporary debates about gun control—to disrupt America's status quo on guns.

OUT OF THE SHADOWS: EMBRACING STUDENT AND TEACHER ACTIVISM'S REJECTION OF THE A NATION AT RISK PARADIGM

Like the student and teacher activism in the 1960s and '70s, the 2018 student protests and teacher strikes were part of a larger national and international pattern of societal disruption. In the United States since the economic recession of the late 2000s, there have been a number of popularized large-scale protest movements, from Occupy Wall Street and the Tea Party to Black Lives Matter and the Women's March (Jaffe, 2016). Additionally, the 2018 student and teacher movements in the United States are also part of larger movements both in the United States and across the world that are rejecting the ideologies that have coalesced to form the A Nation at Risk paradigm in the United States (Horn, 2014; Kennelly, 2014; Pease-Alvarez & Thompson, 2014; Picower, 2012). Students in Tunis, Cairo, Paris, Athens, London, Montreal, and New York have all engaged in activism to challenge the impacts of neoliberalism (Giroux, 2013). In one telling example, in 2006, Chile experienced its largest protest movement since transitioning to an electoral democracy in 1990 when high school students protested inequalities caused by the country's neoliberal school choice system (Kubal & Fisher, 2016). Teachers around the world are also rejecting neoliberalism and its impacts on education. For example, Mexico experienced nationwide teacher strikes and protests in 2016 in opposition to neoliberal education reforms (Bocking, 2018). Like the students and teachers that came before them, the 2018 activists had plenty of company as they sought to challenge the status quo.

Also like the students and teachers before them, the 2018 activists influenced and supported each other. The spring of 2018 was full of teachers supporting and protesting with their students against gun violence and students protesting on behalf of their teachers for greater pay and school funding. In one prominent example, during his speech at the March for Our Lives in Washington, DC, on March 24, Ryan Deitsch (MSD class of 2018) subverted a controversial conservative policy prescription:

> We cannot make America safe again until we arm our teachers. We need to arm our teachers. We need to arm them with pencils, pens, paper, and the money they need! They need that money to support their families and to support themselves before they can support the futures and those classrooms! To support the future that sits at that desk waiting to learn. (March for Our Lives, 2018, p. 166)

This cross-pollination of support for teachers and their struggles was echoed by students across the country who protested alongside their teachers in support of their demands. As one Tucson, Arizona, student proclaimed at a student-led sister protest to #RedForEd, "My teachers have stood for me, and now I will stand for them on the picket line" (Blanc, 2019, p. 79). For their part, teachers supported the burgeoning student protest movement against gun violence both by cultivating student civic agency through their teaching and also joining them in walking out. While it is tempting to see the student protests and teacher strikes of the spring of 2018 as two distinct social phenomena that happened to occur at the same time, they were deeply connected as each group supported, participated in, and inspired each other's actions.

Finally, in addition to drawing support and inspiration from each other, the students and teachers of 2018 drew support from—and were understood within—larger societal movements for social justice. The students of March for Our Lives explicitly modeled their advocacy after the Women's March (Whitney & Duff, 2018). Additionally, both protest movements connected their activities to those of the civil rights movement of the 1960s. The teachers continued traditions of civil disobedience in the face of laws that outlawed strikes by public employees (Blanc, 2019). The students were understood and understood themselves as the natural successors of the civil rights movement and the student protests of the 1960s and '70s. As three of the student cofounders of March for Our Lives expressed:

> We can't begin to say how many times old people that we meet in the street have compared the March for Our Lives movement to the Civil Rights movement and the people that protested the Vietnam War; some of the greatest changes in our history were brought about by young Americans who were sick of not having their voices heard. Even the one and only John Lewis compared us to himself, and told us to keep stirring up "good trouble," and Dr. Martin Luther King

Jr.'s family has given us nothing but support. These are leaders whom we have learned about in school, people whom we emulate in so many ways. Courageous young people throughout history have yelled so loud that it turned the country upside down. Our goal is to do the same. (Barnitt et al., 2018, p. 47)

In these ways, the 2018 students and teachers were the natural successors of a long tradition of civic engagement by these groups in the United States.

Looking back, then, the student protests and teacher strikes of 2018 appear inevitable. They echo a strong history of student and teacher civic activism in the United States. From this perspective, discontent over decades of disinvestment in education and mass shootings at schools finally boiled over and created the next generation of civic activists. But these protests occurred within the A Nation at Risk paradigm that has dominated educational policy since 1983. Within this paradigm, the politics of education are structured in such a way as to deny the participation of students and teachers. The paradigm's "thin" vision of democracy and the ways it redefines civic participation impedes activism like that demonstrated by the students and teachers of 2018. And yet these movements happened as students and teachers collaborated within shadow spaces and reshaped the politics of education to reject the policy outcomes of the A Nation at Risk paradigm and disrupt the ways in which it positions them within educational policy.

CHAPTER 6

Embracing Student and Teacher Civic Agency and Reclaiming "Education for Citizenship"

The student protests and teacher strikes of 2018—and those that have followed—directly oppose the A Nation at Risk paradigm both in its policy outcomes and the ways in which it positions students and teachers within educational policy. Because of this rejection, the activities of these students and teachers offer a natural foundation through which to explore an educational paradigm opposed to the A Nation at Risk paradigm, one that recenters and prioritizes the democratic aims of education over those of private consumerism.

Since 1983, the A Nation at Risk paradigm has dominated educational policy, leading to policies and politics that align with its tenets (Mehta, 2013). Perhaps most significantly, though, it has also reshaped the accepted aims of education in the United States and redefined the conception of citizenship in our democratic society. The A Nation at Risk paradigm elevates, centralizes, and privatizes educational policy decisions (Henig, 2013), while directing education toward the production of individual social capital (Spring, 2011). As expressed in policy, this has led to tighter accountability measures for students, teachers, and schools, the criminalization of school discipline, the narrowing of the curriculum, and a loss of community control over educational decisions. Ultimately, this paradigm leads to a prioritization of education as a private consumer good rather than a public civic good (Mirra & Morrell, 2011). This has led to a thin, market-focused version of democratic citizenship in which democratic deliberation is replaced with consumer choice (Apple, 2018). From within this paradigm, the only proper aim of education is to educate students to engage in the economy and to improve their economic competitiveness within a highly stratified market economy. Other valid aims of education—like preparing students for democratic citizenship—are neglected. This leads to an educational system dominated by private interests that fails to prepare students for their future roles as democratic citizens and not just as future participants in the economy.

Embracing student and teacher civic activism begins to correct this imbalance by both recentering the democratic aims of education and cultivating an educational policy paradigm that requires, rather than discourages, robust democratic deliberation on educational policy and the proper aims of education. Contemporary student and teacher activism, like that of the students and teachers in the spring of 2018, rejects the A Nation at Risk paradigm and embodies the civic agency necessary for democratic citizenship. Because of this, these protests offer a natural starting place to explore an alternative policy paradigm in opposition to the A Nation at Risk paradigm. What would an educational policy paradigm theorized from these activities look like? At their core, these students and teachers are engaging in the messy work of deliberative democracy. By striking, marching, advocating, lobbying, registering voters, petitioning, and walking out, they are collectively engaged in reshaping their social experiences through the democratic process. They are exercising their civic agency. Their actions provide a foundation from which to begin to explore the contours of an educational policy paradigm that supports the development of this civic agency. Building from student protests and teacher strikes like those of 2018, we are able to articulate the foundations of an "Education for Citizenship" paradigm.

Like student and teacher civic activism, an Education for Citizenship paradigm would center civic agency and align with deliberative democratic theories that advance a conception of citizenship founded on civic agency. Within deliberative democratic theory, democratic self-governance is the result of collective decision-making based on public deliberation (Gutmann & Thompson, 2004). In this way, democracy is more than the aggregation of personal self-interest. Instead, it is a collaborative enterprise in which people must deliberate with each other and work together to engage in what Gutmann (1987) calls the "conscious social reproduction" of society. Within this framework, civic agency is a necessary component of citizenship; it is required in order for citizens to be able to engage in the collective work of deliberative democracy.

Deliberative democracy has at its core the value of equality. This flows from the basic idea that all people who are equally bound by the outcomes of the democratic process ought to be politically equal in the process of arriving at those outcomes (Dahl, 1998). Drawing on deliberative democracy, equality should be the animating value of an Education for Citizenship paradigm, just as it was for the 2018 student and teacher activists. These activists celebrated political equality in how they organized and in how they sought to gain equal access to deliberative processes that had excluded their voices. Within the shadow spaces that incubated student and teacher activism, these students and teachers used inclusive, deliberative spaces like social media and Facebook groups to discuss strategies and goals. These spaces were largely open to all, and access was not based on political ideology or adherence to any predetermined policy positions. The teacher protests specifically, in being inclusive of other school personnel beyond just teachers, practiced this value by including all those who are impacted by educational policy decisions. Students, too, practiced equality in their organizing, given the decentralized and horizontal structures that promoted these nationwide protests and their focus on engaging in debate and dialogue around policy prescriptions. Similarly, both the students and teachers, in reorganizing the politics of education under the A Nation at Risk paradigm, also practiced equality by remedying disparities in the deliberative process. These groups were bound by the decisions that impacted educational policy, but, prior to their activism, they were unable to participate in them on equal footing.

Building from equality as its guiding value, an Education for Citizenship paradigm would center preparation for citizenship as the principle aim of public education. Equality within deliberative democracy is focused on ensuring that all citizens are able to engage in the deliberative processes of popular self-governance. This requires both procedural equality, meaning equal access to deliberative democratic processes, and substantive equality, which requires that all citizens have the ability to engage in the deliberative process, utilize their civic agency, and realize their individual and collective goals within the conscious social reproduction of society. An Education for Citizenship paradigm would be primarily directed toward ensuring this substantive strain of equality. Under this paradigm, education would be structured so as to prepare all students to be capable of engaging within deliberative democracy. This echoes Gutmann's (1987) call for a democratic threshold for education that "imposes a moral requirement that democratic institutions allocate sufficient resources to education to provide all children with an ability adequate to participate in the democratic process" (p. 136). Such an education would need to prepare students to be productive citizens. This would include the skills, knowledge, and dispositions necessary to engage in deliberative democracy—such as cognitive autonomy; sufficient content knowledge to understand and grapple with issues of public concern; the ability to make, evaluate, and respond to arguments within deliberation; and a commitment to engage in and respect the outcomes of the deliberative process (Newman, 2013). Most importantly, an Education for Citizenship paradigm, in order to realize the substantive equality of future citizens, would ensure that students were prepared to exercise their civic agency with and alongside others as they work to realize their personal and collective goals. These are the traits of civic agency that contemporary student and teacher activists model so well.

Like student and teacher civic activism, an Education for Citizenship paradigm would also necessarily reject the tenets, policy positioning, and policy outcomes of the A Nation at Risk paradigm (see Table 6.1). While economic goals of education would not be absent from an Education for Citizenship paradigm, they would be mediated through the goal of preparing

Table 6.1. A Comparison of the A Nation at Risk Paradigm and an Education for Citizenship Paradigm

	A Nation at Risk paradigm	Education for Citizenship paradigm
Underlying ideologies	Neoliberalism, neoconservativism, and authoritarian populism	Deliberative democracy
Animating value	Efficiency	Equality
Societal goal	Fostering economic competition through free market capitalism to maximize societal efficiency	Popular self-governance through robust and representative public discourse
Mechanism for achieving its goal	The free market	Deliberative democratic processes
Conception of citizens	Consumers of government	Active participants in and coconstructors of local, national, and global communities
Goal of education	Human capital development	Cultivating active citizenship and civic agency
Makers of educational policy	Centralized political and economic elites	Local school leaders, teachers, students, and citizens through democratic processes
Positioning of students and teachers within educational policy	Students as products of education; teachers as passive policy martyrs	Students and teachers as civic agents
Educational Policy Prescriptions	School choice; standardized tests; a college- and career-ready curriculum; national educational standards; annual yearly progress; merit pay for teachers; zero-tolerance policies	An inclusive curriculum that is responsive to students' identities; service learning; coconstructed curriculum; restorative justice

students for participation in a democratic society. Rather than focusing on being "career ready," this paradigm would focus on being "citizen ready," which includes being a productive member of our national economy. Additionally, an Education for Citizenship paradigm would reject the A Nation at Risk paradigm's "thin" conception of democracy and its positioning of citizens as consumers of government in favor of a "thick" conception of democracy in which citizens are positioned as active coparticipants in the conscious social reproduction of society through the deliberative process. This means that an Education for Citizenship paradigm would endorse the shift of policy decisions away from political elites and private entities toward more responsive and participatory democratic institutions. Thus, like the student and teacher civic activism of 2018, an Education for Citizenship paradigm would oppose the policy prescriptions of the A Nation at Risk paradigm and the ways in which it positions students and teachers as passive recipients of educational policy.

In sum, an Education for Citizenship paradigm would privilege the democratic goals of education to prepare students to be active and effective participants within our democratic society. This would mean providing students and teachers with the opportunities to develop their civic agency and to practice it within educational spaces. An education that provides students the skills, knowledge, and dispositions of civic agency and citizenship would be insufficient if that education did not also allow students—and by extension their teachers—opportunities to develop that civic agency through meaningful engagement with decisions that directly impacted their experiences. Thus, this paradigm repositions students and teachers as cocreators of educational policy rather than the passive recipients of it. Under an Education for Citizenship paradigm, students and teachers would be understood as civic agents. Flowing from this, educational policy decisions would be decentralized away from elites and the federal government toward local democratic bodies, where local school leaders, teachers, students, parents, and community members would have greater voice in educational policy decisions. Ultimately, given an Education for Citizenship paradigm's emphasis on democratic competence and the development of civic agency, all school practices and policies would be evaluated against this metric to see how they advance these goals. This would require a rethinking of curriculum, pedagogy, and the ways in which schools are organized and governed. The next section begins this work, identifying broad policy shifts and criteria for policy decisions that, if embraced, would move educational policy away from the A Nation at Risk paradigm and toward an Education for Citizenship paradigm.

TOWARD REALIZING AN EDUCATION FOR CITIZENSHIP PARADIGM

By embracing the promise of student and teacher activism, school leaders and educational policymakers can work to realize an Education for Citizenship paradigm in educational policy. This shift requires a change in how we think about educational policy. Paradigms create policy, but they also shape how we think about policy. In order to realize an Education for Citizenship paradigm in the face of the currently dominant A Nation at Risk paradigm, at least five broad shifts would need to take place. School leaders and educational policymakers would need to adopt and implement policies that (1) interrupt the crime control paradigm and its punitive approach to student behavior; (2) empower students in their own learning by respecting them as rights holders and future citizens; (3) protect and promote teacher collective agency; (4) engage students, teachers, parents, and local, state, and national communities in the collaborative work of creating educational policy; and (5) center democracy at the heart of teaching and learning. Each of these shifts encompasses concrete policy changes away from the A Nation at Risk paradigm, but, more broadly, they constitute changes in how we ought to think about educational policy.

Interrupt the Crime Control Paradigm and Its Punitive Approach to Student Behavior

The crime control paradigm that characterizes how schools approach student discipline and behavior under the A Nation at Risk paradigm severely limits student civic agency. Students within this paradigm are constantly under surveillance, their actions are severely controlled, and their compliance with externally created rules and norms is enforced through punitive punishments like exclusionary discipline. Students are thus passive, controlled, and—more often than not—the objects of discipline rather than participants in cultivating a productive school culture. This teaches students to be passive recipients of state-sponsored control rather than coproducers of their social reality. To realize a shift away from this paradigm and toward an Education for Citizenship paradigm, school leaders and educational policymakers should institute a more collaborative, restorative, and ultimately more educational approach to school discipline (Black, 2016). In approaching policy under this shift, policymakers and school leaders must ask how they are understanding student behavior and how they are responding to students in ways that prepare them for their future as democratic citizens.

Under the A Nation at Risk paradigm, student misbehavior is viewed as a willful, and therefore culpable, rejection of established and legitimate authority. Absent from this perspective, however, is a recognition of the educational aspects of discipline for students' development as well as an understanding of the causes of student misbehavior and the ways in which student behavior is a function of how schools are structured and organized. In essence, the A Nation at Risk paradigm focuses on modifying students and their behavior to engender compliance with existing school structures as if students are fully rational adults. In doing so, it ignores the impact of school structures and their responsibility for contributing to student behaviors in schools.

An Education for Citizenship paradigm would shift this understanding of student behavior. It would recognize that students are children with developmental needs and that school structures ought to also be responsive to students rather than students alone being held responsible to modify themselves to the needs of their schools. This view requires school leaders and policymakers to consider what students need as individuals and to think through, in collaboration with students, how school structures can be modified to better equip students to engage in acceptable behavior while participating effectively in the school's educational mission. In this way, an Education for Citizenship paradigm welcomes student civic agency by positioning students as active participants in school governance. Students become agents of school discipline rather than merely the objects of it. This prepares students for their future roles as citizens, who will be coresponsible for working with others to engage in the conscious social reproduction of society.

One way in which schools can realize this shift is through restorative justice models of school discipline. Restorative justice shifts the emphasis of school discipline away from "getting even" to "getting well" (Mullet, 2014, p. 158). It does this by prioritizing restorative approaches to misbehavior that focus on addressing the harm caused by the individuals' actions rather than exclusionary punishment that often exacerbates or fails to address this harm. Ironically, by focusing on the causes and effects of student behavior rather than on its deterrence, restorative justice echoes some of the recommendations offered by the original *A Nation at Risk* report. Ultimately, restorative justice seeks to repair relationships between the affected parties to address the causes of problematic behavior. To do this, it (1) gives voice to those affected by misbehavior, including both the harmed and the harmer; (2) encourages accountability by asking those involved to take responsibility for the consequences of their actions and understand how their actions impacted others; and (3) seeks to reintegrate both the harmed and the harmer back into the community by thinking through what those involved can do to better cultivate a caring climate for everyone (Mullet, 2014). In this way, restorative justice cultivates student voice and emphasizes social engagement over social control, both of which are important for developing student civic agency (Morrison & Vaandering, 2012). However, to fully realize an Education for Citizenship paradigm, restorative justice policies would need to both emphasize student voice and accept that, within the complicated interplay of students and schools, schools must also shift their behaviors in response to student voice based on the ways in which schools themselves are responsible for student conduct.

As applied to student and teacher activism, the shift away from punitive approaches to school discipline would affect how school leaders and policymakers respond to student protests. From within an Education for Citizenship paradigm, student protest would be seen as an important expression of student voice—even where it violates the school's rules when, for example, students walk out of school without permission. School leaders would need to attend to why students are protesting in order to dialogue and work with students to determine if changes in the school's structure or culture are necessary. School leaders would need to ask, "What is it about the school's policies that led these students to protest, and what can be done, consistent with the school's educational mission, to address it?" This does not mean that students who break school rules to protest would be free from punishment or that students, through protest, would have veto power over the policies of the school. But it would require that school officials communicate with students about why policy decisions are made, including the decision of whether to punish students for violating the school's rules to protest. In this way, schools would respect student voice and position them as emerging citizens with valuable perspectives that ought to be considered within educational policy.

Empower Students in Their Own Learning by Respecting Them as Rights Holders and Future Citizens

The A Nation at Risk paradigm denies students their agency and voice by making them passive recipients of educational policy and knowledge rather than their cocreators. Not only does this lead to classroom environments that impede students' motivation to learn, but it also fails to respect the future citizenship of students and to acknowledge that students are themselves important stakeholders in educational policy. Each of these consequences undermines the development of student civic agency; students learn that their voices are unwelcome and unnecessary in collective decision-making around policies that directly impact their lives.

To remedy this, an Education for Citizenship paradigm requires school leaders and educational policymakers to ask how their actions position students as participants in their own learning and how students can be respected as rights holders in ways that enable them to actively participate in school governance. From within an Education for Citizenship paradigm, schools need to create democratic spaces for students to engage with the educational policy decisions of schools and with larger social issues (Apple & Beane, 2007). Doing so affirms the importance of students' perspectives on educational policy and social issues that directly impact students' lives— like gun control—and also creates spaces where students can practice and develop civic agency. This does not mean handing control of schools and learning over to students, but it does mean distributing authority in schools more evenly among students, teachers, and administrators. From within this paradigm, students ought to have a voice in what they learn, how they learn it, and the policies and practices around which schools are organized. Doing so not only helps students become more invested in school and succeed academically (Goodman, 2010), it also respects the democratic aims of schooling and allows schools to create structured spaces in which to cultivate student agency.

Hand in hand with cultivating student agency to impact educational decisions, an Education for Citizenship paradigm would require that schools respect students as rights holders and future citizens who are empowered to engage in democratic processes around educational policy and other social issues. Legally protected rights are often the hallmark of citizenship. These rights provide the individual with a sphere of autonomy from which to pursue their conception of the good life. In addition, they also mediate the individual's relationship with the state by constraining what the state may do to the individual. Under the A Nation at Risk paradigm, though, students' rights have been eroded as they have become subordinated to other interests. While students still retain formal legal rights, these rights are often viewed within the A Nation at Risk paradigm as impediments or obstacles rather than essential features of an education for civic agency and democratic citizenship. This further solidifies the position of students as passive recipients of schooling.

Embracing students' rights, like students' free speech and privacy rights, begins to change this and repositions students as active participants in their schooling. These rights balance the relationship between schools and students and allow students the spaces within which to develop their civic agency as they participate in school governance. As future citizens, students will one day have full legal rights. While some might balk at giving students spaces in school to practice exercising their rights and develop their civic agency, it is contradictory to deny students their rights in the very institutions that society has tasked with preparing them to understand and exercise those rights in the future. While the age and maturity of children as well as the school context may justify modifications of students' rights (Warnick, 2013), the goal of cultivating student civic agency requires that students be given at least developmental rights that both honor their future status as citizens and prepare them to understand, value, and exercise those rights outside of the school context in the future. Schools can begin to do this by teaching students directly about their rights, by being explicit in how students' rights influence and inform their actions and policies, and by creating spaces where students can exercise and explore the contours of their rights as they develop their civic agency to impact educational policy decisions.

For student protests, this shift toward respecting students as rights holders who ought to be involved in decisions on educational policy would require school leaders and policymakers to respect students' rights to express themselves through civic protest. Under an Education for Citizenship paradigm, school officials should allow student protests since students are deeply affected by educational policy decisions and have an important and unique perspective that ought to be recognized. However, this would not mean that school officials would be powerless to discipline students who engage in such protests depending on the circumstances. School officials could punish students for violating rules that are applicable to all students and that don't specifically single out students for punishment based on the exercise of their rights. This balances students' rights with the school's legitimate interest in realizing its educational mission, while directing that educational mission toward the development of students' civic agency. For example, school officials could not forbid students from engaging in a protest but could punish students for violating a generally applicable school rule that prohibits students from being out of the classroom without an excuse. In this way, students are respected as future—and current—rights holders, and they are able to develop their civic agency as they work to impact educational policy through their activism.

Protect and Promote Teacher Agency

The A Nation at Risk paradigm doesn't just constrain student civic agency; it also limits teacher agency and positions teachers as passive policy martyrs. This paradigm requires teachers to accept more responsibilities and burdens while it simultaneously cuts funding and lowers teachers' salaries. When coupled with concerted assaults on teachers' collective action and the elevation, centralization, and privatization of educational policy, the A Nation at Risk paradigm requires that teachers do more with less and leaves them with fewer political avenues to influence these outcomes (Anderson & Cohen, 2018). Thus, the only options available to teachers are to stay in teaching and sacrifice their own well-being for the good of their students or leave the teaching profession altogether (Dunn, 2018). Ultimately, this leads both to high rates of teacher attrition as teachers leave the profession and to constrained civic agency for those teachers who remain. This in turn impacts the development of students' civic agency as they lose out on important role models and as tighter systems of control force teachers to engage in more restrictive teaching practices to comply with the A Nation at Risk paradigm's external accountability measures.

In contrast to the A Nation at Risk paradigm, under an Education for Citizenship paradigm, teachers would be important participants in democratic deliberation surrounding educational policy. Teachers—like their students—have an important perspective in creating and implementing educational policy. Thus, within an Education for Citizenship paradigm, educational leaders and policymakers must ask how their actions recognize teachers as active policy agents with valuable experiences and perspectives that ought to inform educational policy (Anderson & Cohen, 2018).

Mirra and Morrell (2011) argue that positioning teachers as active policy agents views teachers as "engaged in learning that is collective, productive, and active" and as members of a "collective endeavor with their students to read the word and the world by engaging in shared inquiry that is embedded in the concerns of the local communities" (p. 413). Such a view of teachers positions them as public intellectuals with important perspectives and expertise on teaching and learning. These teachers actively engage in and seek to shape public discourse, especially around education. This requires teachers to model civic agency as they seek to foster it in their students. Thus, when teachers are understood as civic agents rather than passive conduits of official knowledge, "highly effective teachers are those who support the development of agency within learners and themselves, those who deliberate about issues, those who strategically direct their thoughts and actions in light of goals, and those who act as co-creators" (Boyte & Finders, 2016, p. 145). This view of teachers is in direct conflict with the A Nation at Risk paradigm's view of effective teaching, which sees effective teaching as more efficiently imparting greater amounts of externally validated knowledge to students. Embracing an Education for Citizenship view of teachers opens up possibilities for the development of both student and teacher civic agency and for a renewed and reinvigorated public discourse on education and educational policy.

This view of teachers as active civic agents requires school leaders and educational policymakers to respect teacher collective agency as expressed through teacher unions and teacher strikes. From within an Education for Citizenship paradigm, teachers have an important voice in educational policy, and they ought to be afforded avenues within which to express their perspectives. Thus, the means that teachers use to amplify their voices, like teacher unions, ought to be embraced to the extent that they allow teachers to engage in public intellectualism around educational issues and help teachers to engage in democratic processes around educational policy. This also means that educational policymakers should embrace teacher strikes as a legitimate expression of teacher collective action to influence educational policy, especially when—as was the case in the spring of 2018—those teacher strikes are directed at impacting educational policy at the state level where there is less of a conflict between teacher professionalism and the democratic control of local school districts. As with student civic agency, there is an important balance to be struck between recognizing teacher agency and voice within democratic deliberations over educational policy and allowing those voices to dominate or exert disproportionate influence over those deliberations or their outcomes. Within an Education for Citizenship paradigm, the voices of students, teachers, school leaders, parents, and the larger community must all be recognized within democratic deliberation on educational policy.

Engage Students, Teachers, Parents, and Local, State, and National Communities in the Collaborative Work of Creating Educational Policy

The A Nation at Risk paradigm shifts educational policy decisions away from local, democratic bodies and toward more centralized, and often privatized, decision-makers (Henig, 2013). Thus, under this paradigm, more and more educational policy is made at the state or federal level, and these policies often result in relinquishing educational policy decisions to private corporations or individuals who act as the consumers of education, like with the proliferation of school choice policies. In addition, it also leads to fewer educational decisions being made by education-specific governing bodies, like local and state school boards. Instead, educational policy is set by general-purpose governing bodies like mayors, governors, legislatures, and even courts, causing educational policy to become less democratically accountable. By centralizing educational policy, educational policymakers under the A Nation at Risk paradigm are distanced from the impacts of their decisions and those affected by them. In addition, the influence of educational policy decisions on elected officials is more diffuse as education becomes just one relevant policy domain among many by which to evaluate elected officials. Finally, due to privatization, many educational decisions are not directly accountable to democratic institutions at all except through the policies that privatized those decisions in the first place.

An Education for Citizenship paradigm seeks to correct this imbalance by localizing educational policy, where appropriate, and ensuring that educational policy decisions are accountable to democratic processes rather than private actors. This paradigm recognizes education as a public good that ought to be accountable to the public. Education is the primary public vehicle in our society through which community and national cultures, values, traits, and dispositions are inculcated in future citizens. As such, parents and local, state, and national communities all have important perspectives that ought to be recognized within educational policy, alongside those of students, teachers, and educational leaders.

To realize this goal, school leaders and educational policymakers should consider both (1) whether their actions are the result of an inclusive deliberative process reflecting, as closely as appropriate, those directly affected and (2) how their actions influence who will make educational policy in the future. These considerations raise three important challenges, however. First, what substantive constraints does an Education for Citizenship paradigm place on the outcomes of the democratic process in determining educational policy? Second, how should conflicts between individual preferences and the outcomes of the democratic process be navigated, especially as related to parents and their ability to raise their children as they see fit? And third, recognizing that local, state, and national communities all have a valid interest in education, what is the proper level at which educational policy decisions should be made?

To address the first question, while an Education for Citizenship paradigm properly recognizes that educational policy decisions ought to be the result of robust democratic processes, the outcomes of the democratic process would be limited by the paradigm's educational aim of preparing future citizens for equal participation in our democratic society. Gutmann (1987) argues that the only justification for a nonneutral education is if all parties affected by educational policy participate equally in its development, either now or in the future. From this, Gutmann concludes that students, who typically do not participate in formal democratic processes, are entitled to an education that at a minimum prepares them for their future participation as equal citizens. Under an Education for Citizenship paradigm, with its commitment to political equality, this would require substantive limits on the outcomes of democratic governance in order to protect and promote the future political equality of children. Without substantive limits on the sorts of education that can result from the deliberative process, there would be no guarantee that children would be politically equal as adults. Gutmann relies on this argument to endorse a democratic threshold, a minimum level of education available to all children that prepares them for their future citizenship, as well as the principles of nondiscrimination and nonrepression, all of which limit the substantive outcomes of the democratic process on educational policy decisions.

The principles of nondiscrimination and nonrepression can be seen as protecting two aspects of political equality: procedural equality or equality of access and substantive equality or equality of participation. Nondiscrimination involves an individual's ability to access democratic institutions by guaranteeing that all children receive an education sufficient to prepare them to engage with these institutions (Gutmann, 1987, p. 45). The second, nonrepression, encompasses the equality of individuals within those institutions. It prevents "the state . . . from using education to restrict rational deliberation of competing conceptions of the good life and the good society" (p. 44). While equality of access and equality of participation are both crucial components of political equality that ought to be protected for children during their education, this account fails to fully address how these limits will be enforced to limit the outcomes of the democratic process (Newman, 2013). To resolve this, the democratic threshold and the principles of nondiscrimination and nonrepression can be phrased as two individual, educational rights: (1) a right to an adequate education for democratic citizenship and (2) a right to an equal invitation from public schools. Phrasing these principles as individual rights allows individuals to make—and courts to enforce—moral and legal claims to certain basic educational opportunities that would be inviolable by the democratic deliberative process.

To define the democratic threshold of education, Gutmann and Thompson (1996) rely on the deliberative process. They argue that "the best way of determining what adequacy [of education] practically entails may be a democratic decision-making process that follows upon public debate and deliberation" (p. 137). Such an approach, however, fails to fully account for the role that education plays in preparing individuals for deliberative democracy. Anne Newman (2013) argues that entrusting a democratic threshold of education to the deliberative process ignores the ways in which a lack of education for deliberative democracy can impede effective participation in the deliberative process:

> When individuals in need of the social good at stake are not necessarily politically disadvantaged by that need, deliberatively determining social minimums could yield a fair process and outcome. . . . On the other hand, deprivation of access to an adequate education more often than not converges with the condition of being uneducated in ways that curtail political agency. Deferring to deliberative bodies to decide what constitutes an adequate education, then, renders those citizens most in need of the social good at stake disadvantaged in the very process that should improve their lot. (p. 15)

To remedy this seeming paradox, an Education for Citizenship paradigm would embrace an individual's right to an adequate education for democratic citizenship. Such a right would be enforced by the judiciary—a political branch often semi-insulated from deliberative democracy—and would, like the common law, develop incrementally through a series of legal challenges. At a minimum, the right would guarantee students an education that cultivates students' civic agency and provides students with the skills, traits, and knowledge necessary to engage in the deliberative process of conscious social reproduction.

In addition to the right to an adequate education for democratic citizenship, which promotes equal access to democratic institutions, an Education for Citizenship paradigm would also endorse an individual right to an equal invitation from educational institutions to ensure equal participation within schools. Where a right to an adequate education for democratic citizenship informs the required outcomes of an education, the right to an equal invitation would inform the substance of the child's education. It requires that each student, regardless of their race, class, gender, sexuality, ethnicity, ability, ideology, or any other personal identity, be equally recognized within the school, its structures, policies, and practices—to the extent consistent with an equal invitation for all students.

The concept of an invitation captures this idea. If an individual is allergic to peanuts, and someone invites their friends to tour the factory where they make chocolate peanut butter cups, the allergic individual has not received an invitation equal to that of their friends. There's a disconnect between them and the institution inviting them in that makes the invitation unequal. While this might be acceptable for a private entity in some cases, the same should not be true of public education. There is a growing body of research that demonstrates that students, based on their identities, can be affirmed or alienated from schools based on the practices and content of those schools (Sleeter, 2011). The principle of equal citizenship, which requires that individuals be equal participants in democratic institutions, also requires that these disconnects between schooling and individuals be remedied to the maximum extent possible. This is precisely what the right to an equal invitation protects. It codifies students' moral claim to be equal participants within schools so that they can best receive an education that prepares them to be equal citizens as adults.

Thus, the individual rights to an adequate education for democratic citizenship and an equal invitation from educational institutions constitute substantive limits on the outcomes of the democratic process surrounding educational policy. Within an Education for Citizenship paradigm, these rights protect the future ability of students to engage in the conscious social reproduction of society, while still recognizing the importance of democratic deliberation in determining educational policy.

An Education for Citizenship paradigm also has implications for how to navigate tensions between the results of democratic deliberations and the preferences of parents, communities, and others who have an interest in the education of America's youth. Even with robust participation for parents and communities within democratic deliberation, there is no guarantee that educational policy will reflect the personal preferences of all participants. Indeed, it is likely inevitable, given the value-laden nature of education and child-raising, that some participants will strongly object to the results of the democratic process. While this may be an inevitable result, it becomes problematic when set against a parent's interest in raising their children. To balance these interests, an Education for Citizenship paradigm fully includes parents as participants in public deliberation on educational policy writ large, and it also recognizes parents' authority to influence their individual child's education, though with important limitations.

Under an Education for Citizenship paradigm, parental authority to direct their child's education in ways that conflict with those determined through democratic processes would be limited by the need to prepare students for equal democratic citizenship in the future. Further protecting the child's right to an equal education for democratic citizenship, parents would have the authority to override the results of the democratic process for their child, but only to the extent that it does not interfere with the child's future democratic citizenship. Thus, for example, parents could choose to remove their child from public school due to disagreements with how democratic deliberation has structured that education. But they could not place them in a school that fails to prepare them to engage in democratic deliberation with others who disagree with them. Similarly, parents could not choose to excuse their children from democratically determined curriculum that they find objectionable if doing so would impede the ability of the child to engage in public reason and engage with the ideas of others in public deliberation as future citizens.

This limitation on parental rights echoes Warnick's (2014) argument for a parental "right to invite," in which parents have the right to invite their children into their preferred conception of the good life, but only in ways that do not limit the children's future autonomy. For Warnick, a parental right to invite is founded on the sacrificial labor that parents expend in bearing and raising their children. However, because this sacrificial labor is provided without the consent of the child, parental authority over the child is limited by the need to cultivate the child's future ability to consent. This leads to a right to invite, where parents can invite the child into their way of life but must also cultivate the child's ability to choose among competing ways of life. Within an Education for Citizenship paradigm, parents would have similar authority over their children. They would be able to invite them into their preferred way of life but not in ways that impede the child's ability to develop their future civic agency and equal citizenship.

By providing parents with avenues to participate in their child's education both as citizens engaged in the deliberative democratic process and as parents with important parental rights that ought to be respected by the outcomes of the deliberative process, an Education for Citizenship disrupts the A Nation at Risk paradigm's positioning of parents as mere consumers of education. Under the A Nation at Risk paradigm, because of the ways in which it elevates, centralizes, and privatizes educational policy decisions, parents have educational choice, but this typically means choosing between a selection of existing schools or homeschooling. Within this paradigm, parents are the consumers of education, and much like at a restaurant, they peruse the menu of available school options and choose the one they most prefer for their child. However, because parents are only choosing their child's school, the ability of parents to impact the policies or practices of the schools they ultimately select for their children's education is limited. Indeed, in much the same way the A Nation at Risk paradigm positions students as the passive recipients of educational policy and teachers as passive policy martyrs, the A Nation at Risk paradigm also constrains and redefines parental civic agency. Parents are the consumers of education with no power or authority to affect educational change except through the invisible hand of the market that reflects their aggregate consumer decisions.

The denial of parental civic agency within the A Nation at Risk paradigm can be seen in the recent "parental opt-out" movement. Parents within this movement have "opted out" of having their children take standardized tests either through formal mechanisms or, where no formal mechanisms exist, by simply refusing to send their children to school during testing. As discussed, standardized tests and the accountability regime are outgrowths of the A Nation at Risk paradigm. Parents who engage in the opt-out movement are often doing so out of a deep disagreement with the policy choices and impacts of standardized tests on their students' education (Abraham et al., 2019). However, because the A Nation at Risk paradigm positions parents as consumers of educational policy, parents are unable to challenge these policies within existing forums. The A Nation at Risk paradigm would have them choose a different school, one that better aligns with their policy preferences. Much like teachers who are only given the choice between resigning or continuing to sacrifice themselves under the A Nation at Risk paradigm, parents too are limited in their ability to influence educational policy under it. The parents of the opt-out movement, like student and teacher activists, seized an opportunity that allowed them to reject both the policy outcomes of the A Nation at Risk paradigm and the ways in which it positions them as mere consumers of education (Mitra et al., 2016). In this way, the parental opt-out movement echoes the same rejection of the A Nation at Risk paradigm as student protests and teacher strikes. An Education for Citizenship paradigm would embrace this rejection and instead position parents as democratic participants in educational policy decisions and as authorities over their children's education—with the important caveat that parents do not exercise that authority in ways that impede the child's future civic agency.

The final challenge posed by an Education for Citizenship paradigm and its endorsement of robust public control over educational policy is the question of at which political level decisions about educational policy ought to be made. How should conflicts between local, state, and federal communities be navigated? An Education for Citizenship paradigm requires that educational policy decisions be the result of participatory democratic processes that recognize the voices and perspectives of all impacted stakeholders. Founded on ideas of civic agency and participatory democracy, educational decisions under an Education for Citizenship paradigm ought to be made with as much participation as possible by those most directly impacted by those decisions. However, because state, local, and national communities all have important—yet sometimes disparate—interests in the outcomes of public education, it is difficult to determine at what level educational decisions ought to be made. To help navigate this challenge, an Education for Citizenship paradigm would recognize that educational decisions ought to be made at the lowest or most local level since those communities are the ones most directly impacted by these decisions. However, where important state or national values—like those that inform deliberative democracy—are implicated, the necessity of also involving those communities in educational decision-making would override the local community's interests in the local control of education.

To determine when local control of education ought to give way to greater participation by more diffuse democratic participants, an Education for Citizenship paradigm looks to whether, and to what extent, educational decisions implicate foundational values of deliberative democracy and state and national citizenship. To the extent that national or state values are at stake, educational decisions ought to be made by institutions at those levels that include all the varied stakeholders affected by the realization of those values. Thus, foundational values of democratic citizenship, like political equality or the cultivation of public reason, ought to be mediated by the most diffuse democratic processes at the national level since these are national values at the heart of deliberative democracy. Within this framework, local communities would still have significant control over educational policy decisions, but only to the extent that those decisions do not contradict or limit the realization of more diffuse educational values important to state and national stakeholders.

An Education for Citizenship paradigm's shift toward engaging students, teachers, parents, and local, state, and national communities in the collaborative work of creating educational policy has important implications for how school leaders and policymakers ought to respond to student and teacher activism. First, because these activities correct imbalances in who is recognized within educational policy decisions, these student and teacher activists ought to be welcomed as important participants in the creation of educational policy. Both student and teacher activists are filling gaps created by the A Nation at Risk paradigm in which their collective voices are absent from important educational policy forums that make decisions that deeply impact their lived experiences in schools. An Education for Citizenship paradigm recognizes that educational decisions ought to be made by those most closely affected by those decisions. Because student and teacher civic activism helps realize this goal and shifts educational policy decisions toward local, democratic institutions that are more responsive to democratic participation, these activities should be embraced by school leaders and policymakers.

Second, an Education for Citizenship paradigm would acknowledge that these activities constitute important avenues of political participation for students and teachers and should therefore be protected from limitation by others, especially at the local level. Student protests and teacher strikes are expressions of important national values of citizenship. These activities reify important national values of freedom of speech and public deliberation on issues of public importance. As such, these activities ought to be insulated from local control to the extent that local decisions are inconsistent with promoting these values. Instead, decisions regarding the propriety of these activities ought to be made at more centralized levels of political deliberation, subject of course to the substantive limits offered by the two educational rights discussed.

Lastly, an Education for Citizenship paradigm would recognize the important role that student protests and teacher strikes play in realizing students' future citizenship. Limiting student protests in ways that do not affirm the importance of these activities to the development of students' future citizenship violates students' rights to an adequate education for equal citizenship. Further, because of the ways in which teachers model effective citizenship and the relationship between recognizing teacher agency and teachers teaching in ways that foster student agency, realizing teacher civic agency is equally important to cultivating students' civic agency. For these reasons, the shift of educational policy decisions under an Education for Citizenship paradigm toward robust, local, and participatory democratic processes requires school leaders and policymakers to embrace student and teacher civic activism in ways that affirm these activities and their relationship to students' future citizenship.

Put Democracy at the Heart of Teaching and Learning

The A Nation at Risk paradigm and its emphasis on accountability for economic productivity has narrowed the curriculum, redefined teaching as the transmission of official knowledge, and crowded out meaningful civic education. To counter this, an Education for Citizenship paradigm places democratic citizenship at the core of the educational mission. Within such a paradigm, the principal aim of schooling would be the cultivation of "the values and skills involved in democratic living," such as "respect for human dignity, equity, freedom, and social responsibility, as well as skills like critical thinking, problem solving, collaborating, information and data gathering, reflecting, participatory planning, and the like" (Beane, 2013, p. 10).

Education under an Education for Citizenship paradigm must teach the skills, traits, and knowledge of good citizens—like the skills of cognitive autonomy and public reason—and it must do so within democratic structures that provide opportunities for students to develop, practice, witness, and appreciate democratic modes of governance (Dewey, 1903; Hess & McAvoy, 2015). Without the opportunity to practice democratic self-governance or to witness its importance in schools, it is doubtful that schools will adequately be able to prepare students for democratic citizenship. This means that students must be granted voice, civic agency, and liberty rights to empower them to interact with school officials and policymakers while they are still in school. In addition, teachers and other school personnel should also model active citizenship and allow students spaces to practice their emerging citizenship. This requires embracing the conception of teachers as active civic agents (Mirra & Morrell, 2011), blurring the boundaries between schools and the community (Dewey, 1916/2012), and treating children's education as a conversation between the school, the child, parents, and the community. Not only does this recenter civic agency as a primary goal of public education for students, but it also allows teachers to teach in ways that support autonomy and civic engagement in the classroom. Within an Education for Citizenship paradigm, without the A Nation at Risk paradigm's strict accountability regime aimed toward economic outcomes, teachers could engage in autonomy-supportive teaching that is responsive to students' needs, supports their growth along a variety of dimensions, and allows students space to cultivate and practice their voice (Pelletier & Sharp, 2009).

To accomplish this shift toward an Education for Citizenship paradigm, school leaders and policymakers must ask what aims of education are being promoted through their actions and how they are fostering students' ability to engage equally as citizens in deliberative democracy in the future. These questions recognize that educational policy should center the democratic aims of education by directing education toward the development of future citizens, but it also recognizes that there are other legitimate aims of education within a pluralistic, liberal democratic society (Brighouse et al., 2018).

Importantly, education for democratic citizenship embraces many aspects of other legitimate educational aims. An education for democratic citizenship would necessarily prepare students for deliberative democracy by focusing on cultivating students' abilities to think "critically, reflectively, and independently" (Newman, 2013, p. 35)—all skills that echo the humanistic aims of education, like promoting personal autonomy (Brighouse, 2006) or the cultivation of judgment (Curren, 2014). Students within an Education for Citizenship paradigm would also need to be educated to embrace the sorts of dispositions and values necessary in a democracy, such as equality, freedom, and tolerance, which align well with cultural aims of education, which are directed toward cultivating and deepening students' culture and cultural attachments. Additionally, Noddings (2003) views civic and community participation as an important aspect of happiness—another valid aim of education—a view echoed by Dewey (1916/2012) and his view of democratic ways of life leading to human growth. Finally, democratic citizenship necessarily entails the ability to function productively within our capitalistic society. Thus, an education for citizenship requires that students be educated to be productive members of society's economic life, though not to the exclusion of other goals and with an eye toward participation rather than acquiescence. While not all the aims nor the policies that are informed by each aim are fully consistent with the democratic goals of education, embracing an Education for Citizenship paradigm and placing democracy at the heart of teaching and learning promotes many other aims of education and provides deliberative spaces within which conflicts over other valid aims of education can be mediated—consistent with the development of students' civic agency and their future citizenship.

For student protests and teacher strikes, this shift requires school leaders and educational policymakers to both embrace these examples of civic agency and to do so in ways that affirm their significance to democratic citizenship. Merely allowing these protests without prohibiting them may grant students and teachers the opportunity to practice their civic agency and develop their democratic citizenship, but it does not fully place civic education at the heart of teaching and learning. At best, this sort of approach would acknowledge the civic value of these activities; at worst, it would merely allow but not engage with these protests and fail to grapple with them in an educational way that would affirm the democratic aims of education. Instead, within an Education for Citizenship paradigm, school leaders and educational policymakers confronted with student and teacher activism ought to engage students and teachers in conversations about the role of activism within democracy. This requires centering politics in the classroom rather than excluding it under the mistaken belief that education can be apolitical (Hess & McAvoy, 2015). Additionally, school leaders should listen to students and teachers, including their reasons for protesting and their goals, and allow these groups to participate in creating educational policy moving forward. In this way, school leaders and educational policymakers, in responding to student and teacher civic activism, both affirm the democratic aims of education and inject democratic ideals into how schools are structured. This prepares students for democratic citizenship by teaching them the skills and traits of democratic citizenship and by providing them experiences and role models within schools to help them develop, practice, and appreciate that citizenship.

If schools and educational policymakers embrace these five policy and paradigmatic shifts (see Table 6.2), it would go a long way toward realizing an Education for Citizenship paradigm. Currently, the arc of educational

Table 6.2. Policy Shifts to Realize an Education for Citizenship Paradigm

Required Shift	Animating Question for School Leaders and Educational Policymakers
Interrupt the crime control paradigm and its punitive approach to student behavior.	How are we understanding student behavior, and how are we responding to students in ways that prepare them for their future as democratic citizens?
Empower students in their own learning by respecting them as rights holders and future citizens.	How do our actions position students as participants in their own learning, and how are we respecting students as rights holders in ways that enable students to actively participate in school governance?
Protect and promote teacher collective agency.	How do our actions recognize teachers as active policy agents with valuable experiences and perspectives that ought to inform educational policy?
Engage students, teachers, parents, and local, state, and national communities in the collaborative work of creating educational policy.	How are our actions the result of an inclusive deliberative process reflecting, as closely as appropriate, those directly affected, and how do our actions influence who will make educational policy in the future?
Center democracy at the heart of teaching and learning.	What aims of education are we promoting through this action, and how are we fostering students' ability to engage equally in deliberative democracy in the future?

policy within the A Nation at Risk paradigm is stacked against student and teacher civic agency. Yet, even within this paradigm, there are countertrends and reasons for hope that a paradigmatic shift is possible. Students across the United States who grew up within the A Nation at Risk paradigm still possessed the civic agency necessary to organize one of the largest youth-led protest movements of the last 50 years following the Parkland shooting (Valys et al., 2018). The teachers of West Virginia, Kentucky, Oklahoma, Arizona, Colorado, and North Carolina did the same, even in the face of growing resistance to teachers' collective political activism. Something about these people's lives and education prepared them for these undertakings. The work of those who embrace the democratic aims of education is to identify, understand, and develop the lessons of these protests to reclaim democratic education from the A Nation at Risk paradigm.

CHAPTER 7

The Question Is Not Whether to Respond to Student and Teacher Civic Activism but How

The student and teacher civic activism of the spring of 2018 was just the beginning of a new wave of activism for these groups. Aligning with and continuing larger societal movements, student protests and teacher strikes have continued to gain momentum in the United States and across the world. Because of the teacher strikes, more workers in the United States protested in 2018 than in any year since 1986 (Van Dam, 2019). After North Carolina's teachers went on strike at the end of the spring of 2018, there have been dozens of teacher strikes across the country as teachers have continued to protest at the district and state level. School districts in California, Illinois, Colorado, Ohio, New York, New Jersey, and Washington have all experienced teacher strikes since the spring of 2018, including large urban districts such as Los Angeles Unified School District, Denver Public Schools, Oakland Unified School District, Sacramento United School District, and Chicago Public Schools. Additionally, Washington, West Virginia, South Carolina, North Carolina, and Oregon have all experienced statewide teacher protests that have built on the momentum of the 2018 statewide teacher strikes (Jacobson, 2019; Wong, 2019). At the same time, since the spring of 2018, students have also engaged in local, national, and even international protests on issues ranging from local mask mandates during the COVID-19 pandemic to climate change.

Including the student protests and teacher strikes of the spring of 2018, the United States in the late 2010s and early 2020s experienced widespread societal protests. During the COVID-19 pandemic in 2020, numerous states were the sites of protest movements in opposition to measures intended to prevent the spread of the disease, including stay-at-home orders, school and business closures, and mask mandates (Budryk, 2020). Beginning at approximately the same time, there were renewed and sustained protests—often aligned with the Black Lives Matter movement—against discriminatory policing and police brutality as over 140 cities across the United States experienced protests following the killing of George Floyd, a Black man, while he was in police custody (Taylor, 2021). Less than 6 months later, in the fall of 2020 into the winter of 2021, the United States experienced a sustained movement to delegitimize the 2020 presidential election, as dozens of states experienced protests and forms of political violence challenging the legitimacy of the election of President Joe Biden, culminating in the January 6, 2021, riot and attack on the U.S. Capitol (Atlantic Council's DFRLab, 2021).

Within this context, students and teachers continued to engage in civic activism, building from both the 2018 student and teacher civic activism and larger societal movements. Teachers following 2018 continued to strike and protest for greater compensation and increased school funding. In 2019, teachers in Texas, Maryland, Florida, Kentucky, West Virginia, California, Illinois, Colorado, and West Virginia, among others, engaged in sustained teacher strikes and protests on these issues. As a result, nearly half of state governors proposed raising teacher pay in 2019 (Will, 2019). In addition to more traditional protests in pursuit of greater legal recognitions and financial concerns, during the COVID-19 pandemic, many teachers and their unions engaged in activism to address what they saw as unsafe plans to return to in-person learning or reopening plans that placed too great a burden on teachers (Beer, 2020).

Students, too, continued to protest and expand their political agenda following the 2018 protests. Following the Parkland protests, the March for Our Lives and the National Student Walkout organizations continue to advocate for gun reform legislation and engage in wide-ranging voter registration and turn-out drives. Indeed, youth voter turnout in the 2020 presidential election increased by 11%, growing from 39% in 2016 to 50% in 2020 (Center for Information & Research on Civic Learning and Engagement, 2021). In addition, emboldened students across the country continued to protest on a wide range of issues, including climate change, responses to the COVID-19 pandemic, and support of their teachers' demands for higher pay and better educational conditions (Barrett, 2019).

Continuing the tradition of national student-led protests, on September 20, 2019, millions of students and young people in the United States and around the world engaged in an international day of activism to protest what they saw as inadequate political responses to the threat of climate change (Sengupta, 2019). These protests were part of a sustained global student strike movement to address climate change (Weise, 2019). In the United States, there were over 1,000 local protests organized by the U.S. Youth Climate Strike Coalition, an organization of eight U.S. youth-led climate groups that united online and began planning the climate protests in June 2019 (Janfaza, 2019). Reporting on the student climate change protests, Sengupta (2019) writes, "Rarely, if ever, has the modern world witnessed a youth movement so large and wide, spanning across societies rich and poor, tied together by a common if inchoate sense of rage." Led by students and young people, who are deeply impacted by environmental policy but who have little formal power to affect it, these protests continued the tradition of student activism that includes those following the 2018 Parkland shooting.

In addition to the climate protests, America's students also joined and promoted national protest movements. Following the killing of George Floyd, students in Minnesota engaged in numerous school walkouts and protests of police violence and the presence of police in schools, which were echoed by students across the country. One prominent organization, Minnesota Teen Activists, used Instagram to organize a statewide student walkout on April 19, 2021, during the murder trial of Derek Chauvin, the officer who knelt on Floyd's neck (Ajasa & Beckett, 2021). This same organization had previously used social media to organize a GoFundMe campaign that raised over $50,000 to assist small businesses impacted by social unrest following Floyd's death (Ajasa & Beckett, 2021). Also mirroring larger national protest movements, students throughout the COVID-19 pandemic protested both for and against various COVID-19 protocols and school reopening plans. For example, students in Ann Arbor, Michigan, organized a rally in front of their high school to protest their district's decision to remain virtual through the 2020–2021 school year (Bruckner, 2021). In another illustrative example, students in Tomahawk, Wisconsin, engaged in a walkout of a school assembly regarding the school's policy requiring all individuals on school grounds to wear masks (Maki, 2021).

As the history of student and teacher activism and the activities of students and teachers since the spring of 2018 demonstrate, the 2018 student protests and teacher strikes were not an anomaly. Students and teachers have a long history of activism, and that tradition has continued through 2018 and beyond. In the face of persistent student and teacher civic activism, the question for teachers, school leaders, and educational policymakers is not whether to respond to these activities but how.

As has been true throughout American history, responses to contemporary student and teacher civic activism have been mixed. Many school leaders and community members have been supportive of these protests, including joining protestors in their activities or choosing not to discipline students or teachers for their activism. Others, however, have sought to tamp down student and teacher activism by threating to punish students and fire teachers who engage in these activities. On the legislative front, while not aimed specifically at student and teacher civic activism, in the early months of 2021, more than 80 antiprotest bills were introduced in 34 states, largely in response to the ongoing protests against police brutality and discriminatory policing following the George Floyd killing and the Black Lives Matter movement (Castronuovo, 2021). While this was a marked rise in antiprotest legislation, between November 2016 and June 2021, 45 states considered 226 bills aimed at restricting the right to peacefully assemble (International Center for Not-For-Profit Law, n.d.). These bills may have had larger societal protests in their crosshairs, but many of them were at least informed by student and teacher activism. Among these bills, some of the penalties for criminalized conduct included preventing convicted individuals from receiving student loans (Sheffey & Zeballos-Roig, 2021) or from holding employment with a state educational institute or receiving a state professional license, such as a teaching license (Castronuovo, 2021).

Not all legislative efforts have been exclusively antiprotest, however. At least one state, Virginia, after bipartisan advocacy from student groups, passed a law allowing middle and high school students to miss 1 day during the school year to engage in a civic or political event (Cherner, 2021). In addition, at both the state and federal level, a renewed emphasis on civics education has begun to emerge. In 2021 alone, more than 34 states considered bills to promote civics education (Vasilogambros, 2021). At the national level, one proposed bill, the Civics Secures Democracy Act of 2021, would invest $1 billion annually for 6 years to promote civic education (Coons, 2021). While these bills have often received bipartisan support, the exact contours of civic education remain a hotly debated issue (Packer, 2021). In many ways, conflict over the content and form of civics education mirrors the conflict between the A Nation at Risk paradigm and an Education for Citizenship paradigm. From the perspective of the A Nation at Risk paradigm, civic education—where pursued at all—ought to teach students how government works and instill allegiance to existing institutions, which for the state is often expressed as an uncritical form of patriotism. From within this framework, civics education is less about participating in civic life and more about inculcating students to acquiesce and accept the results of governmental policies that promote neoliberal and neoconservative ideologies. From the Education for Citizenship paradigm, however, civics education is primarily focused on cultivated civic agency, the ability to work with others to shape public policy and our shared experiences. This results in a civics education that emphasizes active participation in governance over passive acceptance. These two perspectives on civics education align with contemporary political discourse—compare, for example, the Trump administration's *1776 Commission Report* (The President's Advisory 1776 Commission, 2021) and its emphasis on uncritical, patriotic education to the *Roadmap to Educating for American Democracy* (Educating for American Democracy, 2021) and its emphasis on "reflective patriotism" and political participation. At the very least, these conflicts indicate the potential for an educational paradigm that privileges student and teacher civic agency in opposition to the A Nation at Risk paradigm.

These legislative efforts and public debates about the nature of civics education demonstrate that, in response to contemporary student and teacher civic activism, some educational policymakers and school leaders have sought to double down on the A Nation at Risk paradigm. These efforts seek to further solidify a policy environment that endorses a passive conception of student and teacher civic agency while simultaneously—and paradoxically—fostering the conditions that lead students and teachers toward civic activism. On the other hand, since 2018, educational leaders and policymakers have also begun to embrace and learn from these protests—and the traditions of activism that inform them—to think through how these protests offer a new way forward for educational policy, a way that is grounded in student and teacher civic agency that puts an Education for Citizenship at the heart of our schools.

References

Abraham, S., Wassell, B., Luet, K., & Vitalone-Racarro, N. (2019). Counter engagement: Parents refusing high stakes testing and questioning policy in the era of the common core. *Journal of Education Policy, 34*(4), 523–546.

Ajasa, A., & Beckett, L. (2021, April 20). Hundreds join Minneapolis high school walkouts: "Police don't care about us." *The Guardian.* https://www.theguardian.com/us-news/2021/apr/19/minneapolis-st-paul-high-school-student-protest-walkout-daunte-wright-george-floyd

Allen, A. (2006). Changing ties: Charter schools redefine the school-community connection. *Journal of School Public Relations, 27*(1), 84–119.

Alvarez, R. (2003). "There's no such thing as an unqualified teacher:" Unionization and integration in the Philadelphia public schools. *The Historian, 65*(4), 837–865.

Anderson, G., & Cohen, M. (2018). *The new democratic professional in education: Confronting markets, metrics, and managerialism.* Teachers College Press.

Apple, M. (1988). Redefining equality: Authoritarian populism and the conservative restoration. *Teachers College Record, 90*(2), 167–184.

Apple, M. (2005). Doing things the 'right' way: Legitimating educational inequalities in conservative times. *Educational Review, 57*(3), 271–293.

Apple, M. (2006). *Educating the "right" way: Markets, standards, God, and inequality* (2nd ed.). Routledge.

Apple, M. (2014). *Official knowledge: Democratic education in a conservative age* (3rd ed.). Routledge.

Apple, M. (2018). Rightist gains and critical scholarship. *Educational Review, 70*(1), 75–83.

Apple, M., & Beane, J. (2007). Schooling for democracy. *Principal Leadership, 8*(2), 34–38.

Associated Press. (2018a, April 14). In latest victory for protesting teachers, Kentucky increases education spending. *Los Angeles Times.* https://www.latimes.com/nation/nationnow/la-na-kentucky-teachers-20180414-story.html

Associated Press. (2018b, April 30). *Colorado Gov. John Hickenlooper signs $28.9 billion state budget.* Denver Channel. https://www.thedenverchannel.com/news/politics/colorado-gov-john-hickenlooper-signs-289-billion-state-budget

Atlantic Council's DFRLab. (2021, February 10). *#StopTheSteal: Timeline of social media and extremist activities leading to 1/6 insurrection.* Just Security. https://www.justsecurity.org/74622/stopthesteal-timeline-of-social-media-and-extremist-activities-leading-to-1-6-insurrection/

Baker, S. (2011). Pedagogies of protest: African American teachers and the history of the civil rights movement, 1940–1963. *Teachers College Record, 113*(12), 2777–2803.

Ball, S. (2016). Neoliberal education?: Confronting the slouching beast. *Policy Futures in Education, 14*(8), 1046–1059.

Barnitt, J., Chadwick, S., & Whitney, S. (2018). Creating a social media movement: Mid to late February. In March for Our Lives (Ed.), *Glimmer of hope* (pp. 39–48). Razorbill & Dutton.

Barrera, J. (2004). The 1968 Edcouch-Elsa High School walkout: Chicano student activism in a south Texas community. *Aztlan, 29*(2), 93–122.

Barrett, D. (2019). How youth activism has changed the country in the year since Parkland. *Teen Vogue*. https://www.teenvogue.com/story/youth-activism-changed-the -country-in-the-year-since-parkland

Baumgartner, F., & Jones, B. (1993). *Agendas and instability in American politics.* University of Chicago Press.

BBC News. (2019, August 5). *America's gun culture in charts.* https://www.bbc.com /news/world-us-canada-41488081

Beane, J. (2013). A common core of a different sort: Putting democracy at the center of the curriculum: The values and skills associated with life in a democratic society should constitute the core of the curriculum. *Middle School Journal, 44*(3), 6–14.

Beckett, L. (2019, February 14). Parkland one year on: What victories have gun control advocates seen? *The Guardian.* https://www.theguardian.com/us-news/2019 /feb/14/parkland-school-shooting-anniversasry-gun-control-victories

Beer, T. (2020, August 16). Teachers organize mass sick days, resignations, and potential strikes over schools reopening. *Forbes.* https://www.forbes.com/sites /tommybeer/2020/08/16/teachers-organize-mass-sick-days-resignations-and -potential-strikes-over-schools-reopening/?sh=62b53d253fe1

Beger, R. (2002). Expansion of police power in public schools and the vanishing rights of students. *Social Justice, 29*(1), 119–130.

Ben-Porath, S. (2013). Deferring virtue: The new management of students and the civic role of schools. *Theory and Research in Education, 11*(2), 111–128.

Bethel School District v. Fraser, 478 U.S. 675 (1986).

Bidgood, J. (2018, March 6). West Virginia raises teachers' pay to end statewide strike. *The New York Times.* https://www.nytimes.com/2018/03/06/us/west -virginia-teachers-strike-deal.html

Black, D. (2016). *Ending zero tolerance: The crisis of absolute school discipline.* New York University Press.

Blackford, L. (2018, February 2). Kentucky teachers storm the Capitol: "We have no choice but to be here." *Lexington Herald Leader.* https://www.kentucky.com /news/politics-government/article207682419.html

Blanc, E. (2019). *Red state revolt: The teachers' strike wave and working-class politics.* Verso.

Blount, J. (2017). Ella Flagg Young and the gender politics of *Democracy and Education. Journal of the Gilded Age and Progressive Era, 16,* 409–423.

Board of Ed. of Independent School Dist. No. 92 of Pottawatomie Cty. v. Earls, 536 U.S. 822 (2002).

Bocking, P. (2018). The Mexican teachers' movement in the context of neoliberal education policy and strategies for resistance. *Journal of Labor and Society, 22,* 61–76.

Boren, M. E. (2001). *Student resistance: A history of the unruly subject.* Routledge.

Bourdieu, P., & Passeron, J. (1990). *Reproduction in education, society and culture.* (2nd ed., R. Nice, Trans.). SAGE.

Boys join strikers: More students at San Francisco leave school to protest against teachers riding on cars. (1917, October 10). *Los Angeles Times*, p. 14.

Boyte, H., & Finders, M. (2016). "A liberation of powers": Agency and education for democracy. *Educational Theory, 66*(1–2), 127–145.

Brax, R. (1981). *The first student movement: Student activism in the United States during the 1930s.* Kennikat.

Brent, J. (2016). Placing the criminalization of school discipline in economic context. *Punishment & Society, 18*(5), 521–543.

Brighouse, H. (2006). *On education.* Routledge.

Brighouse, H., Ladd, H., Loeb, S., & Swift, A. (2018). *Educational goods: Values, evidence, and decision-making.* The University of Chicago Press.

Brown, R. (1996). *The strength of a people: The idea of an informed citizenry in America, 1650–1870.* University of North Carolina Press.

Brown v. Board of Education, 347 U.S. 483 (1954).

Brownlee, W. (1979). *Dynamics of ascent: A history of the American economy.* Knopf.

Bruckner, M. (2021, February 19). *Ann Arbor high school students to protest Saturday, demand return to schools.* All About Ann Arbor. https://www .clickondetroit.com/all-about-ann-arbor/2021/02/19/ann-arbor-high-school -students-to-protest-saturday-demand-return-to-schools/#//

Budryk, Z. (2020, May 3). Governors, experts await results of reopening states as protests continue. *The Hill.* https://thehill.com/homenews/sunday-talk -shows/495877-governors-experts-await-results-of-reopening-states-as-protests

Bundy, T. (2017). "Revolutions happen through young people!": The Black student movement in the Boston public schools, 1968–1971. *Journal of Urban History, 43*(2), 273–293.

A burlesque on strikes: Pupils of a parochial school in Brooklyn catch the contagion. (1886, March 18). *The New York Times*, p. 8.

A burlesque on strikes: Pupils of a parochial school in Brooklyn catch the contagion. (1886, March 28). *Chicago Daily Tribune*, p. 11.

Callahan, R. (1964). *Education and the cult of efficiency: A study of the social forces that have shaped the administration of the public schools.* The University of Chicago Press.

Callan, E. (2000). Liberal legitimacy, justice, and civic education. *Ethics, 111*(1), 141–55.

Campbell, A. (2019, February 19). West Virginia's teachers are on strike again: Here's why. *Vox.* https://www.vox.com/2019/2/19/18231486/west-virginia-teacher -strike-2019

Cano, R., Atlevena, L., Longhi, L., & Beard Rau, A. (2018, April 26). Thousands of teachers, supporters walk out for more educational funding. *AZCentral.* https://www.azcentral.com/story/news/local/arizona-education/2018/04/26 /arizona-teacher-walkout-redfored-education-funding/548892002/

Castronuovo, C. (2021, April 21). 34 states considering anti-protest bills introduced by Republicans: Report. *The Hill.* https://thehill.com/homenews /state-watch/549495-34-states-considering-anti-protest-bills-introduced-by -republicans

Center for Information & Research on Civic Learning and Engagement. (2021, April 29). *Half of youth voted in 2020, an 11-point increase from 2016.* https://circle.tufts.edu/latest-research/half-youth-voted-2020-11-point-increase-2016

Cherner, J. (2021, March 30). *Students successfully lobby for a new state law excusing them from school to protest.* ABC News. https://abcnews.go.com/Politics/students-successfully-lobby-state-law-excusing-school-protest/story?id=76736167

Chuck, E., Johnson, A., & Siemaszko, C. (2018, February 14). *17 killed in mass shooting at high school in Parkland, Florida.* NBC News. https://www.nbcnews.com/news/us-news/police-respond-shooting-parkland-florida-high-school-n848101

Cohen, A., Azrael, D., & Miller, M. (2014, October 15). Rate of mass shootings has tripled since 2011, Harvard research shows. *Mother Jones.* https://www.motherjones.com/politics/2014/10/mass-shootings-increasing-harvard-research/

Cohen, R. (1997). *When the old left was young: Student radicals and America's first mass student movement, 1929–1941.* Oxford University Press.

Colored pupils on strike. (1886, October 20). *The New York Times,* p. 2.

Coons, C. (2021, March 11). *Sens Coons, Cornyn and Reps. DeLauro, Cole, Blumenauer introduce bipartisan, bicameral bill to expand access to and strengthen civics education.* Office of Senator Chris Coons. https://www.coons.senate.gov/news/press-releases/sens-coons-cornyn-and-reps-delauro-cole-blumenauer-introduce-bipartisan-bicameral-bill-to-expand-access-to-and-strengthen-civics-education

Cowles, L. (2014). A seat at the table: Women teachers and the domestication of politics in Chicago. *American Educational History Journal, 41*(2), 313–325.

Cox, J., Rich, S., Chiu, A., Muyskens, J., & Ulmanu, M. (2019, May 8). Database of school shootings. *The Washington Post.* https://www.washingtonpost.com/graphics/2018/local/school-shootings-database/

Curren, R. (2014). Judgment and the aims of education. *Social Philosophy & Policy Foundation, 31*(1), 36–59.

Dagenais, F., & Marascuilo, L. (1972). Student demonstrations in a multiracial high school: The case of Berkeley. *Youth and Society, 3*(4), 457–476.

Dahl, R. (1998). *On democracy.* Yale University Press.

Danns, D. (2002). Black student empowerment and Chicago: School reform efforts in 1968. *Urban Education, 37*(5), 631–655.

Danns, D. (2003). Chicago high school students' movement for quality public education, 1966–1971. *Journal of African American History, 88*(2), 138–150.

Darling-Hammond, L. (2010). *The flat world and education: How America's commitment to equity will determine our future.* Teachers College Press.

Dee, T. (2004). Are there civic returns on education? *Journal of Public Economics, 88*(9–10), 1697–1720.

Delli-Carpini, M., & Keeter, S. (1996). *What Americans know about politics and why it matters.* Yale University Press.

DenHoed, A. (2018, April 4). Striking Oklahoma teachers win historic school-funding increase and keep on marching. *The New Yorker.* https://www.newyorker.com/news/news-desk/striking-oklahoma-teachers-win-historic-school-funding-increase-and-keep-on-marching

Dewey, J. (1903). Democracy in education. *Elementary School Teacher, 4,* 193–204.

Dewey, J. (2012). *Democracy and education.* Simon & Brown. (Original work published in 1916)

Dinkes, R., Cataldi, E., & Lin-Kelly, W. (2007). *Indicators of school crime and safety: 2007.* National Center for Education Statistics. https://nces.ed.gov /pubs2008/2008021a.pdf

District of Columbia v. Heller, 554 U.S. 570 (2008).

Donahue, D. (2002). Rhode Island's last holdout: Tenure and married women teachers at the brink of the Women's Movement. *History of Education Quarterly, 42*(1), 50–74.

Dunn, A. (2018). Leaving a profession after it's left you: Teachers' public resignation letters as resistance amidst neoliberalism. *Teacher College Record, 120,* 1–34.

Educating for American Democracy. (2021). *Educating for American democracy: Excellence in history and civics for all learners.* https://www.educatingfor americandemocracy.org/wp-content/uploads/2021/02/Educating-for-American -Democracy-Report-Excellence-in-History-and-Civics-for-All-Learners.pdf

Elk, M. (2018, May 16). In North Carolina, 20,000 skip school as teachers strike movement swells. *The Guardian.* https://www.theguardian.com/education/2018 /may/16/north-carolina-teachers-strike-low-pay-poor-funding-schools

Fabelo, T., Thompson, M., Plotkin, M., Carmichael, D., Marchbanks, M., & Booth, E. (2011). *Breaking schools' rules: A statewide study of how school discipline relates to students' success and juvenile justice involvement.* Counsel of State Governments Justice Center. https://csgjusticecenter.org/wp-content /uploads/2020/01/Breaking_Schools_Rules_Report_Final.pdf

Falkowski, M. (2018). Getting to work on the newspaper. In M. Falkowski & E. Garner (Eds.), *We say #NeverAgain: Reporting by the Parkland student journalists* (pp. 10–13). Crown.

Falkowski, M., & Garner E. (Eds.). (2018). *We say #NeverAgain: Reporting by the Parkland student journalists.* Crown.

Fear of teacher strike prompted Loeb rule. Attorney Shannon argues that affiliation with labor federation would bring trouble. (1916, February 4). *Chicago Daily Tribune,* p. 18.

Fisher-Ari, T., Kavanagh, K. & Martin, A. (2017). Urban teachers struggling within and against neoliberal, accountability-era policies. *PennGSE Perspectives on Urban Education, 13*(2), 1–19.

Fishlow, A. (1966). The American common school revival: Fact or fancy? In H. Rosovsky (Ed.), *Industrialization in two systems* (pp. 40–67). Wiley.

Florida Department of Education. (n.d.). *2019–20 Marjory Stoneman Douglas High School report card.* https://edudata.fldoe.org/ReportCards/Schools.html?school =3011&district=06

Frederick, R., & View, J. (2009). Facing the rising sun: A history of Black educators in Washington, DC, 1800–2008. *Urban Education, 44*(5), 571–607.

Freire, P. (1970). *Pedagogy of the oppressed.* Seabury.

Fuentes, A. (2003). Discipline and punish: Zero tolerance policies have created a "lockdown environment" in schools, *The Nation, 277,* 17–20.

Garner, E. (2018). Finding the light. In M. Falkowski & E. Garner (Eds.), *We say #NeverAgain: Reporting by the Parkland student journalists* (pp. 15–18). Crown.

Garza, M. (1990, May 6). After long years of calm, student protests are back. *Chicago Tribune,* pp. A1, A6.

Gegax, T., Adler, J., & Pederson, D., (1998, April 6). Schoolyard killers. *Newsweek, 131,* 20–26.

Gillen, J. (2009). An insurrectionary generation: Young people, poverty, education, and Obama. *Harvard Educational Review, 79*(2), 363–369.

Giroux, H. (2013). The Quebec student protest movement in the age of neoliberal terror. *Social Identities, 19*(5), 515–535.

Glass, R. (1967, August). Work stoppages and teachers: History and prospect. *Monthly Labor Review*, 43–46.

Goldin, C., & Katz, L. (1999). Human capital and social capital: The rise of secondary schooling in America, 1910–1940. *Journal of Interdisciplinary History, 29*(4), 683–723.

Goldstein, D., & Dias, E. (2018, April 12). Oklahoma teachers end walkout after winning raises and additional funding. *The New York Times*. https://www.nytimes.com/2018/04/12/us/oklahoma-teachers-strike.html

Goodman, J. (2010). Student authority: Antidote to alienation. *Theory and Research in Education, 8*(3), 227–247.

Graham, G. (2006). *Young activists: American high school students in the age of protest*. Northern Illinois University Press.

Gray, S. (2018, April 18). Everything you need to know about the April 20 National School Walkout. *Time*. http://time.com/5238216/national-school-walkout-april-20/

Grim student war threatens: Order anent class meetings stirs rebellion. (1908, November 5). *Los Angeles Times*, p. II9.

Grinberg, E., & Muaddi, N. (2018, March 26). *How the Parkland students pulled off a massive national protest in only 5 weeks*. CNN. https://www.cnn.com/2018/03/26/us/march-for-our-lives/index.html

Goss v. Lopez, 419 U.S. 565 (1975)

Gutierrez, H. (1996). Racial politics in Los Angeles: Black and Mexican American challenges to unequal education in the 1960s. *Southern California Quarterly, 78*(1), 51–86.

Gutmann, A. (1987). *Democratic education*. Princeton University Press.

Gutmann, A., & Thompson, D. (1996). *Democracy and disagreement*. Belknap.

Gutmann, A., & Thompson, D. (2004). *Why deliberative democracy?* Princeton University Press.

Hale, J. (2013). "The fight was instilled in us": High school activism and the Civil Rights Movement in Charleston. *The South Carolina Historical Magazine, 114*(1), 4–28.

Hale, J. (2018a). Future foot soldiers or budding criminals?: The dynamics of high school student activism in the southern black freedom struggle. *The Journal of Southern History, 84*(3), 615–652.

Hale, J. (2018b). "The development of power is the main business of the school": The agency of southern black teacher associations from Jim Crow through desegregation. *The Journal of Negro Education, 87*(4), 444–459.

Haley, M. (2006). The factory system. In K. Knight Abowitz & R. Karaba (Eds.), *Readings in sociocultural studies in education* (pp. 9–18). McGraw-Hill.

Hall, D., & McGinity, R. (2015). Conceptualizing teacher professional identity in neoliberal times: Resistance, compliance and reform. *Education Policy Analysis Archives, 23*(88), 1–17.

Hall, P. (1993). Policy paradigms, social learning, and the state: The case of economic policymaking in Britain. *Comparative Politics, 29*, 275–296.

Harrison, B. (1993). Roots of the anti-Vietnam war movement. *Studies in Conflict and Terrorism, 16*, 99–111.

Hazelwood v. Kuhlmeier, 484 U.S. 260 (1988).

Heilbron, R. (1974). Student protest at its best: San Diego, 1918. *The Journal of San Diego History, 20*(1). http://www.sandiegohistory.org/journal/1974/january/protest/

Henig, J. (2013). *The end of exceptionalism in American education.* Harvard University Press.

Herbst, J. (1996). *The once and future school: Three hundred and fifty years of American secondary education.* Routledge.

Hess, D., & McAvoy, P. (2015). *The political classroom: Evidence and ethics in democratic education.* Routledge.

Hinnant-Crawford, B. (2016). Education policy influence efficacy: Teacher beliefs in their ability to change education policy. *International Journal of Teacher Leadership, 7*(2), 1–27.

Hirschfield, P. (2008). Preparing for prison?: The criminalization of school discipline in the USA. *Theoretical Criminology, 12*(1), 79–101.

Hirschfield, P., & Celinska, K. (2011). Beyond fear: Sociological perspectives on the criminalization of school discipline. *Sociology Compass, 5*(1), 1–12.

Hodges, T. (2018, April 4). *Teachers seek more input in school decision-making.* Gallup. https://news.gallup.com/poll/232142/teachers-seek-input-school-decision-making.aspx

Hogg, D., & Hogg, L. (2018). *#NeverAgain: A new generation draws the line.* Random House.

Horn, B. (2014). Moments or a movement?: Teacher resistance to neoliberal education reform. *Forum, 56*(2), 277–286.

Horton, A. (2018, April 15). Kentucky governor apologies for comments suggesting kids were sexually assaulted while teachers protested. *The Washington Post.* https://www.washingtonpost.com/news/education/wp/2018/04/14/kentucky-governor-claims-that-children-were-raped-used-drugs-while-teachers-protested

Hutchinson, B. (2018, April 24). As 10,000 teachers plan to descend on Colorado capitol, lawmakers propose jailing them if they go on strike. ABC News. https://abcnews.go.com/US/10000-teachers-plan-descend-colorado-capitol-lawmakers-propose/story?id=54662604

International Center for Not-For-Profit Law. (n.d.). *US protest law tracker.* https://www.icnl.org/usprotestlawtracker/

Jacobson, L. (2017, October 11). *Counting up how much the NRA spends on campaigns and lobbying.* Politifact. https://www.politifact.com/truth-o-meter/article/2017/oct/11/counting-up-how-much-nra-spends/

Jacobson, L. (2019, August 29). *Tracker: Teachers on strike.* Education Dive. https://www.educationdive.com/news/tracker-teachers-on-strike/547339/

Jaffe, S. (2016). *Necessary trouble: Americans in revolt.* Nation Books.

Janfaza, R. (2019, September 19). *Inside the youth-led plan to pull off the biggest climate strike so far.* MTV News. http://www.mtv.com/news/3139644/inside-the-youth-led-plan-to-pull-off-the-biggest-climate-strike-so-far/

Janus v. American Federation of State, County, and Municipal Employees, Council 31, 585 U.S. __ (2018).

Johnston, A. (2015). Student protests, then and now. *Chronicle of Higher Education, 62*(16), 13.

Justice Policy Institute. (2011). *Education under arrest: The case against police in schools.* http://www.justicepolicy.org/uploads/justicepolicy/documents/educationunderarrest_fullreport.pdf

Kasky, C. (2018). How it all began: February 14th. In March for Our Lives (Ed.), *Glimmer of hope* (pp. 1–9). Razorbill & Dutton.

Kennelly, J. (2014). The Quebec student protests: Challenging neoliberalism one pot at a time. *Critical Arts, 28*(1), 135–139.

Knox v. Service Employees International Union, 567 U.S. __ (2012).

Koyama, J. (2017). Competing and contested discourses on citizenship and civic praxis. *Educational Policy Analysis Archives, 25*(28), 1–23.

Kubal, M., & Fisher, E. (2016). The politics of student protest and education reform in Chile: Challenging the neoliberal state. *The Latin Americanist, 2016,* 217–241.

Kuhn, C. (2018, April 11). *Arizona's teachers 'walk-in' to protest low pay and low funding.* NPR. https://www.npr.org/2018/04/11/601419914/arizona-teachers-to-protest-low-pay-and-school-funding-shortfalls

Kuhn, T. (1962). *The structure of scientific revolutions.* The University of Chicago Press.

Kupchik, A., & Monahan, T. (2006). The new American school: Preparation for post-industrial discipline. *British Journal of Sociology of Education, 27*(3), 617–631.

Leachman, M., Masterson, K., & Figueroa, E. (2017, November 29). *A punishing decade for school funding.* Center on Budget and Policy Priorities. https://www.cbpp.org/research/state-budget-and-tax/a-punishing-decade-for-school-funding

Legro, J. (2000). The transformation of policy ideas. *American Journal of Political Science, 44,* 419–432.

Levinson, M. (1999). *The demands of liberal education.* Oxford University Press.

Lipman, P. (2011). *The new political economy of urban education: Neoliberalism, race, and the right to the city.* Routledge.

Loder-Jackson, T. (2015). *Schoolhouse activists: African American educators and the long Birmingham civil rights movement.* SUNY Press.

Magee, M. (2001, May 1). The big question: Who should patrol schools? *The San Diego Union-Tribune,* 1B.

Mahanoy Area School District v. B.L., 594 U.S. ___ (2021).

Maki, J. (2021, May 13). *Students walk out of school in protest after assembly on mask policy.* Merrill Foto News. https://merrillfotonews.com/2021/05/13/students-walk-out-of-school-in-protest-after-assembly-on-mask-policy/

Mann, H. (1849). *The Massachusetts system of common schools: Tenth annual report of the Massachusetts Board of Education.* https://archive.org/details/massachusettssys01mass

March For Our Lives. (n.d.-a). *Mission statement.* https://marchforourlives.com/mission-statement

March For Our Lives. (n.d.-b). *It ends with us: A plan to reimagine public safety.* https://marchforourlives.com/peace-plan/

March for Our Lives. (2018). *Glimmer of hope.* Razorbill & Dutton.

McDonald v. Chicago, 561 U.S. 742 (2010).

McGregor, G. (2018). How "the right" continues to "do wrong" by our young people: Contemporary reflections on Michael Apple's analysis of the "rightist turn" in education. *Educational Review, 70*(1), 84–90.

Mehta, J. (2013). How paradigms create politics: The transformation of American educational policy, 1980–2001. *American Educational Research Journal, 50*(2), 285–324.

Mehta, J. (2015). Escaping the shadow: *A Nation at Risk* and its far-reaching influence. *American Educator, 39*(2), 20–26.

Metzger, D. (2002). Finding common ground: Citizenship education in a pluralistic democracy. *American Secondary Education, 30*(2), 14–32.

Meyer, J., Tyack, D., Nagel, J., & Gordon, A. (1979). Public education as nation-building in America: Enrollments and bureaucratization in the American states, 1870–1930. *American Journal of Sociology, 85*(3), 591–613.

Min, S. (2015). Occupy Wall Street and deliberative decision-making: Translating theory to practice. *Communication, Culture, & Critique, 8*(1), 73–89.

Mirra, N., & Morrell, E. (2011). Teachers as civic agents: Towards a critical democratic theory of urban teacher development. *Journal of Teacher Education, 62*(4), 408–420.

Mitra, D., Mann, B., & Hlavacik, M. (2016). Opting out: Parents creating contested spaces to challenge standardized tests. *Education Policy Analysis Archives, 24*(31). https://doi.org/ 10.14507/epaa.24.2142

The modern schoolboy: Pupils of south Boston strike for shorter hours. (1886, April 21). *The Atlanta Journal-Constitution*, p. 1.

Morrison, B., & Vaandering, D. (2012). Restorative justice: Pedagogy, praxis, and discipline. *Journal of School Violence, 11*, 138–155.

Morse v. Frederick, 551 U.S. 393 (2007).

Mullet, J. (2014). Restorative discipline: From getting even to getting well. *Children & Schools, 36*(3), 157–162.

Muncie students strike to raise pay for teachers. (1920, March 18). *Chicago Daily Tribune*, p. 4.

Muñoz, C. (2018). The Chicano movement: Mexican American history and the struggle for equality. *Perspectives on Global Development and Technology, 17*, 31–52.

Murdock, L. (2018). *National high school walk-out for anti gun violence.* Change .org. https://www.change.org/p/u-s-senate-national-high-school-walk-out-for -anti-gun -violence

Murphy, M. (1992). *Blackboard unions: The AFT and the NEA, 1900–1980.* Cornell University Press.

Nation's students "strike" for peace; disorders are few: Thousands at universities in city join protest against war and fascism. (1935, April 13). *The New York Times*, p. 1.

National Center for Educational Statistics. (n.d.). *Total number of public school teachers and percentage of public school teachers in a union or employees' association, by state: 1999–2000, 2003–04, and 2007–08.* https://nces.ed.gov /surveys/sass/tables/sass0708_043_t1s.asp

National Center for Educational Statistics. (2015). *Public school safety and discipline: 2013–14 first look.* U.S. Department of Education.

National Education Association. (2018). *Ranking of the states 2017 and estimates of school statistics 2018.* http://www.nea.org/assets/docs/180413-Rankings _And_Estimates_Report_2018.pdf

National Institute of Education. (1978). *Violent schools—safe schools: The safe school study report to the congress—executive summary.* U.S. Department of Health, Education, and Welfare.

Nasaw, D. (1979). *Schooled to order: A social history of public schooling in the United States.* Oxford University Press.

Neem, J. (2018). Does the Common Core further democracy? *Democracy & Education, 26*(1), 1–4.

Neirynck, R. (1967). Teachers' strikes: A new militancy. *Notre Dame Lawyer, 43*(3), 367–388.

Newman, A. (2013). *Realizing educational rights: Advancing school reform through courts and communities.* The University of Chicago Press.

New Jersey v. T.L.O., 469 U.S. 325 (1985).

Nie, N., Junn, J., & Stehlik-Barry, K. (1996). *Education for democratic citizenship in America.* The University of Chicago Press.

Niemi, R., & Junn, J. (1998). *Civic education.* Yale University Press.

Nir, S. (2018, April 20). 19 years after Columbine, students again say "enough" on gun violence. *The New York Times.* https://www.nytimes.com/2018/04/20/nyregion/student-walkout-gun-violence-new-york.html

Noddings, N. (2003). *Happiness and education.* Cambridge University Press.

Noll, M. (2007). Princeton in the revolutionary era, 1757–1815. *Presbyterian Historical Society, 85*(2), 89–101.

Novak, S. (1977). *The rights of youth: American colleges and student revolt, 1798–1815.* Harvard University Press.

Office for Civil Rights, U.S. Department of Education. (2014, March 21). *Civil rights data collection: Data snapshot: school discipline.* http://ocrdata.ed.gov

Ohlsen, M. (1971). Dissident students. *Contemporary Education, 42*(4), 157–163.

Oxford English Dictionary Online. (2018). *Indignation.* www.oed.com/view/Entry/94496

Packer, G. (2021, May 15). Can civics save America?: Teaching civics could restore health to American democracy, or inflame our mutual antagonisms. *The Atlantic.* https://www.theatlantic.com/ideas/archive/2021/05/civics-education-1619-crt/618894/

Pasadena students get up in revolt: High school pupils protest against hard problems. (1902, June 12). *Los Angeles Times,* p. A7.

Pease-Alvarez, L., & Thompson, A. (2014). Teachers working together to resist and remake educational policy in contexts of standardization. *Lang Policy, 13,* 165–181.

Pelletier, L., & Sharp, E. (2009). Administrative pressures and teachers' interpersonal behavior in the classroom. *Theory and Research in Education, 7*(2), 174–183.

Pickering v. Board of Education, 391 U.S. 563 (1968).

Picower, B. (2012). Teacher activism: Enacting a vision for social justice. *Equity & Excellence in Education, 45*(4), 561–574.

Polletta, F. (1999). "Free spaces" in collective action. *Theory and Society, 28,* 1–38.

Pralle, S. (2003). Venue shopping, political strategy, and policy change: The internationalization of Canadian Forest Advocacy. *Journal of Public Policy, 23,* 233–260.

The President's Advisory 1776 Commission. (2021). *The 1776 Report.* https://trumpwhitehouse.archives.gov/wp-content/uploads/2021/01/The-Presidents-Advisory-1776-Commission-Final-Report.pdf

Pruter, R. (2003). Chicago high school football struggles, the fight for faculty control, and the war against secret societies, 1898–1908. *Journal of Sport History, 30*(1), 47–72.

Ransford, H. (1972). Blue collar anger: Reactions to student and Black protest. *American Sociological Review, 37,* 333–346.

Ravitch, D. (2010). *The death and life of the great American school system: How testing and choice are undermining education.* Basic Books.

Rosenblattt, K., Chuck, E., & Sperling, J. (2018, March 14). *Students demand action on gun violence with nationwide walkout.* NBC News. https://www.nbcnews.com/news/us-news/national-school-walkout-marks-month-parkland-mass-shooting-n856386

Rousmaniere, K. (2005). *Citizen teacher: The life and leadership of Margarat Haley.* SUNY Press.

Rudolph, F. (1965). *Essays on education in the early republic; Benjamin Rush, Noah Webster, Robert Coram, Simeon Doggett, Samuel Harrison Smith, Amable-Louis-Rose de Lafitte du Courteil, Samuel Knox.* Belknap.

Rury, J., & Hill, S. (2013). An end of innocence: African-American high school protest in the 1960s and 1970s. *History of Education, 42*(4), 486–508.

Scribner, C. (2015). Beyond the metropolis: The forgotten history of small-town teachers' unions. *American Journal of Education, 121,* 531–561.

Schinkel, A., de Ruyter, D., & Steutel, J. (2010). Threats to autonomy in consumer societies and their implications for education. *Theory and Research in Education, 8*(3), 269–287.

Schiraldi, V., & Ziedenberg, J. (2001). *Schools and suspensions: Self reported and the growing use of suspensions.* Justice Policy Institute.

Schirmer, E. (2017). When solidarity doesn't quite strike: The 1974 Hortonville, Wisconsin teachers' strike and the rise of neoliberalism. *Gender and Education, 29*(1), 8–27.

Schneid, R. (2018). The role of a journalist: Exposing the epidemic of gun violence. In M. Falkowski & E. Garner (Eds.), *We say #NeverAgain: Reporting by the Parkland student journalists* (pp. 30–33). Crown.

School boys on a strike: They gather in a vacant lot and threaten other pupils. (1886, April 14). *The Boston Globe,* p. 1.

A school on strike: Pupils resenting their teacher's dismissal. (1887, January 26). *The New York Times,* p. 5.

School teachers strike: Twenty-five resign because superintendent is not re-engaged. (1910, May 8). *The New York Times,* p. 20.

School wants tango: Business high pupils protest against ban on dance. (1913, November 28). *The Washington Post,* p. 4.

Seitz, R. (1966). Legal aspects of public school teacher negotiating and participating in concerted activities. *Marquette Law Review, 49*(3), 487–511.

Sengupta, S. (2019, September 20). Protesting climate change, young people take to streets in a global strike. *The New York Times.* https://www.nytimes.com/2019/09/20/climate/global-climate-strike.html?searchResultPosition=48

Sheffey, A., & Zeballos-Roig, J. (2021, April 21). 2 GOP-led states are attempting to bar protesters convicted of crimes from receiving student loans and jobless aid. *Business Insider.* https://www.businessinsider.com/gop-states-protest-student-loans-jobless-aid-bill-minnesota-indiana-2021-4

Shelton, J. (2017). *Teacher strike!: Public education and the making of a new American political order.* University of Illinois Press.

Sherkat, D., & Blocker, T. J. (1994). The political development of sixties' activists: Identifying the influence of class, gender, and socialization on protest participation. *Social Forces, 72*(3), 821–842.

Simon, J. (2006). *Governing through crime: How the war on crime transformed American democracy and created a culture of fear.* Oxford University Press.

Skiba, R., & Rausch, M. (2006). Zero tolerance, suspension, and expulsion: Questions of equity and effectiveness. In C. M. Evertson & C. S. Weinstein (Eds.), *Handbook for classroom management: Research, practice, and contemporary issues* (pp. 1063–1089). Routledge.

Sleeter, C. (2011). *The academic and social value of ethnic studies: A research review.* National Education Association.

Sloan, K. (2008). The expanding educational services sector: Neoliberalism and the corporatization of curriculum at the local level in the US. *Journal of Curriculum Studies, 40*(5), 555–578.

Snow, A., & Tang, T. (2018, May 3). Arizona teachers end walkout after governor signs off on 20 percent raise. *Chicago Tribune.* https://www.chicagotribune.com/nation-world/ct-arizona-teacher-protests-20180503-story.html

Spina, N. (2017). Governing by numbers: Local effects on students' experiences in writing. *English in Education, 51*(1), 14–26.

Spring, J. (2011). *The politics of American education.* Routledge.

Striking San Diego students pass time helping Red Cross: Whole city in turmoil as result of wholesale dismissals of high school teachers: Civic organizations protest to the Board of Education. (1918, June 16). *Los Angeles Times,* p. II3.

Strober, M., & Tyack, D. (1980). Why do women teach and men manage? A report on schools. *Signs, 5*(3), 494–503.

Strom, D. (1979). Teacher unionism: An assessment. *Education and Urban Society, 11*(2), 152–167.

Students were winners: End of Lawrence Academy strike: Principal Hayward resigns and the school reopens today. (1889, January 23). *The Boston Globe,* p. 8.

Swanchak, J. (1972). Student radicals and the high school. *The Educational Forum, 36*(3), 373–381.

Tarr, D. (2018). Speaking for those who can't. In M. Falkowski & E. Garner (Eds.), *We say #NeverAgain: Reporting by the Parkland student journalists* (pp. 58–61). Crown.

Taylor, D. (2021, March 28). George Floyd protests: A timeline. *The New York Times.* https://www.nytimes.com/article/george-floyd-protests-timeline.html

Teachers defiant in student strike. (1936, October 1). *The Washington Post,* p. X6.

Teachers may strike, too: Cudahy instructors threaten to join their pupils in protest on superintendent's ousting. (1927, November 12). *Los Angeles Times,* p. 1.

Teachers' strike off: Law comes to aid fifteen young women who went out at Pittston. (1902, March 26). *The New York Times,* p. 9.

Thapliyal, N. (2018). #Eduresistance: A critical analysis of the role of digital media in collective struggles for public education in the USA. *Globalisation, Societies and Education, 16*(1), 49–65.

Thornton, R. (1982). U.S. teachers' organizations and the salary issue: 1900–1960. *Research in Economic History, 1982*(2), 127–143.

Tinker v. Des Moines Independent Community School District, 393 U.S. 503 (1969)

Toloudis, N. (2019). Pennsylvania's teachers and the tenure law of 1937. *The Journal of Policy History, 31*(2), 217–241.

Turner, C., Lombardo, C., & Logan, E. (2018, April 25). *Teacher walkouts: A state by state guide*. NPR. https://www.npr.org/sections/ed/2018/04/25/602859780/teacher-walkouts-a-state-by-state-guide

Urban, W. (1993). The making of a teachers' union: The National Education Association, USA, 1957–1973. *Historical Studies in Education, 5*(1), 33–53.

Urofsky, M. (Ed.). (1970). *Why teachers strike: Teachers' rights and community control*. Anchor Books.

Valys, P., Geggis, A., & Chokey, A. (2018, March 14). National walkout day: Students from Stoneman Douglas and across U.S. call for safety, gun control. *Sun Sentinel*. http://www.sun-sentinel.com/local/broward/parkland/florida-school-shooting/fl-florida-school-shooting-walkouts-20180314-story.html

Van Dam, A. (2019, February 14). Teacher strikes made 2018 the biggest year for worker protest in a generation. *The Washington Post*. https://www.washingtonpost.com/us-policy/2019/02/14/with-teachers-lead-more-workers-went-strike-than-any-year-since/

Van Dyke, N. (1998). Hotbeds of activism: Locations of student protest. *Social Problems, 45*(2), 205–220.

Vasilogambros, M. (2021, May 19). *After Capitol riot, some states turn to civics education*. Pew. https://www.pewtrusts.org/en/research-and-analysis/blogs/stateline/2021/05/19/after-capitol-riot-some-states-turn-to-civics-education

Vernonia v. Acton, 515 U.S. 646 (1995).

Wald, J., & Thurau, L. (2010). *First do no harm: How educators and police can work together more effectively to keep schools safe and protect vulnerable students*. Charles Hamilton Houston Institute for Race and Justice.

Walker, V. (2005). Organized resistance and Black educators' quest for school equality, 1878–1938. *Teachers College Record, 107*(3), 355–388.

Walker, V. (2013). Tolerated tokenism, or the injustice in justice: Black teacher associations and their forgotten struggle for educational justice, 1921–1954. *Equity & Excellence in Education, 46*(1), 64–80.

Warnick, B. (2013). *Understanding student rights in schools: Speech, religion, and privacy in educational settings*. Teachers College Press.

Warnick, B. (2014). Parental authority over education and the right to invite. *Harvard Educational Review, 84*(1), 53–71.

Weise, E. (2019, September 19). "It's our future that's at stake": US students plan to skip school Friday to fight climate "emergency." *USA Today*. https://www.usatoday.com/story/news/nation/2019/09/19/climate-strike-us-students-skip-school-fight-climate-change/2368349001/

West Virginia v. Barnette, 319 U. S. 624 (1943).

White pupils walk out in race protest. (1949, February 2). *The Washington Post*, p. 7.

Whitney, S., & Duff, B. (2018). Becoming a team: February 15 and 16. In March for Our Lives (Eds.), *Glimmer of hope* (pp. 13–21). Razorbill & Dutton.

Will, M. (2019). Across the nation, more teachers are protesting with broader sets of demands. *Education Week*. https://www.edweek.org/teaching-learning/across-the-nation-more-teachers-are-protesting-with-a-broader-set-of-demands/2019/03

Wisconsin: Pupils strike for a holiday and get it. (1886, June 1). *Chicago Daily Tribune*, p. 6.

Wisconsin v. Yoder, 406 U.S. 205 (1972).

Women's March. (n.d.). *Mission and principles.* https://womensmarch.com/mission-and-principles

Women's March. (2019, February 28). *Women's March Youth Empower announces Enough! Youth Week of Action.* https://womensmarch.com/press-releases/march-11-15-womens-march-youth-empower-announces-enough-youth-week-of-action?rq=guns

Wong, A. (2018, February 28). West Virginia's teachers are not satisfied. *The Atlantic.* https://www.theatlantic.com/education/archive/2018/02/west-virginia-teachers-strike/554546/

Wong, A. (2019, January 22). America's teachers are furious: From West Virginia to Los Angeles, educators are ushering in a new era of labor activism. *The Atlantic.* https://www.theatlantic.com/education/archive/2019/01/teachers-are-launching-a-rebellion/580975/

Wright, D. (2003). Black Pride Day, 1968: High school student activism in York, Pennsylvania. *Journal of African American History, 88*(2), 150–162.

Yan, H. (2018, May 29). *Here's what teachers accomplished with their protests this year.* CNN. https://www.cnn.com/2018/05/29/us/what-teachers-won-and-lost/index.html

Index

About the Author

Christopher D. Thomas is a practicing attorney with Frost Brown Todd LLC, where he primarily represents local school districts and other governmental entities. Prior to practicing law, Thomas was a high school English teacher. He then returned to school and earned his JD and PhD in educational policy, both from The Ohio State University. Chris lives in Columbus, Ohio, with his wife, Liz; their son, James; and their two cats, Maya and Ruth, the latter of whom is named—of course—after Justice Ruth Bader Ginsburg.